KYFFIN,
A FIGURE IN A
WELSH LANDSCAPE

T0158383

To my incomparable wife, Celia,
who, as in all things, helped, inspired
– and Pip Moss, of the donkey work

KYFFIN,
A FIGURE IN A
WELSH LANDSCAPE

the biography of Sir Kyffin Williams RA,
told through conversations with the artist
and his friends by

Ian Skidmore

seren

Seren is the book imprint of
Poetry Wales Press Ltd
57 Nolton Street, Bridgend, CF31 3AE, Wales
www.seren-books.com

© Ian Skidmore, 2008

ISBN 978-1-85411-463-1

The publisher works with the financial assistance
of the Welsh Books Council.

Printed in Plantin by The Cromwell Press Ltd, Trowbridge

KYFFIN,
A FIGURE IN A
WELSH LANDSCAPE

PROLOGUE

Kyffin Williams painted in Welsh. It could hardly be other. Though he was a product of an English public school, Shrewsbury; soldiered in Northern Ireland, an unlikely officer in the Royal Welch Fusiliers; studied art with the Slade School, evacuated to wartime Oxford; taught it in London, at Highgate School, his antecedents nevertheless form a chain of Welsh gold which glitters down the centuries. The pious, the profane, piratical even. Soldiers and scholars and the downright outrageous were numbered amongst his ancestors. His was less a genealogy than a novel by a Celtic Fielding, all coming together in the complex conundrum that was Wales's greatest living painter and for many years the country's only Royal Academician.

He was heavy with honours. An OBE, Deputy Lieutenant of Gwynedd, M.A., D. Litt, Fellow of three Welsh colleges, President of the Royal Cambrian Academy. Only the second artist to receive the medal of the Honourable Society of Cymrodorion, since its inception in 1880. In the New Year Honours of 1999 he was knighted. Not a bad record for a man who, according to a school report, "is incapable of lucid thought" and who believed with some justice he had never been fully acknowledged by the arts establishment of Wales. It is also true and astonishing that his work was never in his life time chosen for any exhibition of Welsh art which toured overseas. A friend told how he overheard two pillars of the art establishment agreeing that Kyffin was the greatest single threat to Welsh art. Yet the picture-buying public venerates him.

Tall, even in his eighties, an action man with a scholar's stoop; dressed in tweeds as ancient as his lineage, he was the sum of a mass of contrasts. For most of his life he was John Williams. Indeed you could place his friends in context by those who called him John and the later ones to whom he will always be Kyffin. It is a measure of the man that his biographer, though struggling to be impartial, cannot bring himself to identify him by his surname.

His voice, his outlook, the fox hunting, mountain walking way of life were unashamedly elite, unreconstructed *uchelwyr*, the dwindling race of Welsh squires. Yet his paintings, drawings and prints push at the frontiers of art. More, perhaps, than any painter this century he was admired by the public and by his fellow painters. The so-called 'art establishment', the fashionable critics who ignored him, never saw what the people who flocked to his exhibitions saw. They did not realise it was the moustache that was reactionary and the public school accent. The paintings were cutting edge. A perceptive scholar has likened him to Van Gogh, with whom he shared a lifetime in thrall to epilepsy and diabetes. They differ in one important respect. Van Gogh did not sell a picture during his lifetime. Kyffin's pictures sold as fast as his dealers could hang them.

Since 1997, on the night before the opening of his London summer exhibition at the Thackeray Gallery off Kensington Square, potential customers have slept on the street. A queue master was appointed to decide which picture a customer should have. At the 1998 exhibition Kyffin was distressed that many were allowed to buy two which meant that people at the tail end of the queue went home empty handed. Mary Yapp, his Cardiff agent, took a call from a man who was worried he couldn't get down the night before the opening of his 1998 exhibition at her Albany Gallery. He offered £100 to anyone who would stand in for him. The owners of the three galleries where Kyffin exhibited claimed that no other Welsh artist, and few other British artists, have had such an eager public. Interestingly all three owners are women, and all of them surrogate elder sisters to the unworldly Kyffin.

His output was staggering. No picture took him longer than a day to paint and he painted on most days. He was a source of joy and happiness to his friends, wildly generous and deeply caring, with a photographic memory which was an album of outrageous anecdote. Yet he claimed never to have known happiness, and to have lived most of his life on the dangerous frontier of suicide. A frontier his much loved and admired elder brother Richard crossed.

ONE

Kyffin came to art by accident and reluctantly, on the advice of a doctor who in discussing his epilepsy told him he was abnormal. The doctor insisted that on no account should he return to his pre-war occupation as a land agent which would involve sitting examinations. He advised taking up painting, an occupation that would not tax his brain.

In fact, Kyffin had been drawing since the age of two. The subject of his first sketch was his brother Richard sitting on the chamber pot. It earned him a merciless beating with a tortoise-shell hair brush from his prudish mother for being a dirty boy. Understandably he did not want to become a painter and was very upset at the thought of being abnormal. An Irish nursing sister consoled him; "Don't worry about that," she advised. "Sure ninety per cent of the world is abnormal."

It was Kyffin's sense of humour and a monumental awareness of the absurd which saved him. As to being abnormal, there is a country saying which insists you cannot breed tame rabbits from wild ones, and abnormality did not run in Kyffin's line; it danced in high glee. A distant ancestor, a squire of Gogerddan near Aberystwyth named Sir George Pryce, thought if there could be Owen Owens, William Williams and John Johns then why not a Pryce Pryce? He ordered his infant son to be so christened. Unfortunately the officiating vicar was deaf. Given the name the first time he said "I am afraid I cannot quite hear you."

"Pryce," repeated the child's mother.
"I am afraid I cannot quite hear you."
"Pryce," repeated the child's mother more loudly.
Three times.
"I am afraid I cannot quite..."

This was too much for the choleric squire. Standing in his manorial pew he shouted "Pryce, you bloody fool. PRYCE, PRYCE, PRYCE."

This time the vicar heard.

"I christen this child Pryce Pryce Pryce Pryce," he said firmly.

"And so it was," Kyffin always added, building one absurdity onto another "until the poor boy died in consequence of having been bitten by a fox. He was hunting the family's own pack of hounds when a fox went to earth. Pryce Pryce Pryce Pryce went after him and the fox bit him."

Kyffin was at home with all manner and condition of men but his happiest memories were of the farmers of his childhood. He would listen entranced to their stories. Men like Huw Jones of Swtan who told him one day of a bottle which had been found in the chimney of a nearby farm Ty Wion. In it, he said, there had ben found a very old piece of paper with four prophesies written on it:

"The first," he said, "was that a time would come when people would go up in the air and fly like birds. And that has come true, hasn't it?"

The young Kyffin agreed it had.

"The second was that people would go down to the bottom of the sea and swim like fish. And that has come true, hasn't it?"

Once again the young Kyffin agreed.

"And there would come a time when people would talk to each other across continents. And they do, don't they?"

Again Kyffin agreed.

"And the fourth was the date of the end of the world." Huw Jones and his voice grew heavy with apprehension. Alarmed Kyffin leaned forward and asked, "When will that be?"

Farmer Jones looked out of his window and a long silence ensued. At last he turned

"Damn," he said. "I've forgotten."

A childhood friend, Olwen Caradoc Evans, remembered Kyffin as a lonely boy who was always accompanied on his roams round the countryside by his Jack Russell terrier, Bonzo, an outdraft from the Tanatside Hunt. But Olwen also remembered him as the fittest little boy who could run up and down a mountain with ease.

Kyffin's oldest friend was the landowner and founder of the country's largest private forestry business, Roger Williams Evans of Glasfryn on the Lleyn Peninsula. His first memory of Kyffin concerned his childhood skill at drawing.

> I was seven and had been invited to a party at Plas Gwyn which had been taken by the Williamses. We were handed a series of twenty or thirty drawings by Kyffin, who was about twelve, and asked to identify the objects. They must have been well drawn because one was a fountain pen and you had to identify its make.

Seminal to Kyffin's development as an artist was a pack of foxhounds, the Ynysfor; a small private foot pack of six couple. The country they hunted included some of the most glorious mountain scenery in Britain and was certainly the roughest upland hunting. Over Yr Eryri, across Crib Coch, up and down Tryfan and all over the formidable Glyders the followers ran in pursuit of the hounds.

The importance of the Ynysfor Hunt and its members in Kyffin's life cannot be over-stated. No-one painted mountains better and he has said that everything he knows about mountains he learned out hunting with that pack of hounds. It was with the pack that he also met the man who gave him his first lessons in painting.

In time and to his intense surprise painting became more important than staying up with hounds. Enchanted by the panorama in the high mountains he would let the pack run on and stay to capture the picture they made.

Ynysfor gave Kyffin not just his artist's eye. It gave him a family. Rebuffed by his mother, he gloried in this new improbable family in their house above the kennels. It was a house that until Maddocks built his embankment at Porthmadog in the nineteenth century had been on a large island, Ynys Mawr.

Ynys Mawr was a wooded mound a mile long and a quarter of a mile wide with little bays and cliffs. One of the many small islands in a stretch of Wales which until the sea was turned away must have been among the most beautiful bays in Europe. Even now the prospect from Maddocks' embankment to Cnicht mountain, shaped like a Norman helmet, and Yr Eryri beyond is breath-taking and leaves one wishing that Maddocks had left well alone.

The Joneses were among the last of the true North Welsh squirearchy, whose family hunted their own hounds, farmed and lived off their own land for a hundred and fifty years. Not aristocratic. Organic rather. A family which spoke Welsh on the hearth, an old Welsh long forgotten which had forty words for dungheap.

The first Jones to come to Ynysfor over two centuries ago was the son of a Welsh parson. Jackie Jones went to Oxford to read theology but had instead spent his time hunting. He brought to his new home the first pack of rough coated black and tan Welsh hounds. The Hendy, in which he lived, like all old Welsh houses had no view. Beauty in Wales is more often received through the ear rather than the eye. The Hendy was a long low house with a stepped gable into which a small dovecote was built. It overlooked a stable yard and hound kennel. It sheltered below the hill peak from the brisk Snowdonia weather. It had been built with stones which probably came from a Romano-British fort on the crest.

In 1865 Jackie's grandson John built a new house on rising ground facing the peak of the Cnicht. A substantial house with a good sized hall and well windowed rooms.

His son Colonel Evan Jones, a darkly handsome soft spoken man who was known to the girls as Sentimental Evan. He was Master of the Hounds and when he hunted always wore the hunt uniform of brown tweed jacket and breeches with blue facings and a blue velvet waistcoat. Nothing sentimental about his brother Captain Jack who found his girls among the rough and ready country girls in the Maentwrog pub where he drank at nights. Between the brothers were eight sisters. All but one died unmarried. The sweethearts of the other seven were all killed in the First World War. A tragedy no less poignant for being common amongst girls of their age.

Kyffin and Roger were regular visitors. Sixty years on Kyffin remembered those days.

> The Ynysfor family were remarkable. My family had known them for a hell of a long time. I started going out with them I was about 13 or 14. When I started all the Jones sisters came out.

They were pretty tough. One of them Minnie had hunted hounds herself during the first world war. They used to position themselves on hill tops across country. The hounds would find. One sister on her peak would shout to the next sister "Have you seen the hounds?" and that would be relayed to the next sister on her hillock maybe a mile away. And so on until the final sister who might shout "gone into the Cwm" and "Cwwwm!" would echo over miles of countryside. That is how it used to be done. Now it's all done by walkie talkie.

My companions were Roger, Ernest Naish who was a lieutenant in the navy, Cedric Maby who was in the Foreign Office and Harry Glyn, one of the Glyns of Hawarden the family into which the Gladstones married. He was very tall – about 6ft 6 ins. He always said that if he was killed he wanted a stone carved on the summit of Cnicht. In fact he was killed at the first battle of Narvik.

Except for Roger who was younger than me they were all just a little bit older than I was. Very few local Welsh boys went out. It might have been some strange social thing but hunting doesn't seem to be part of the Welsh set up, though the Ynysfors were completely Welsh and of the land.

When I first of all went out hunting I couldn't keep up with Ernest Naish who had very long legs. It was really heavy going because Jack Jones was a terrific walker. An incredible man. Precipices meant nothing to him. I once saw him take hounds across the vertical face of the Craig Ddu in the Cwm Llan above Gwynant in order to drive a fox from a narrow ledge. They had a kennel huntsman Frank Edwards who lived in Cwm Bychan and walked every hunting day ten miles over the mountains to the meet. He would walk and run another twenty to thirty miles out hunting and then in the evening walk home in the dark over the mountains. He was a lovely man.

There was one wonderful old huntsman Harry Jones who was always known as Harry Bet. Bet was his mother who had been a maid in The Goat Hotel in Beddgelert. The story was that Gladstone was staying there. Gladstone and Bet had an assignation and Harry was the result. Certainly Harry was an immensely distinguished man and he looked rather like Gladstone. Everyone looked up to him. There was another huntsman called Evan Go, the blacksmith. He had one eye.

I was always a very nervous boy and kept very much in the background. I was a loner too... My brother Richard was keen on team games but I was happiest wandering the fields with Bonzo and a gun.

My brother was too kind for bloodsports. He came with me

rook shooting and was appaled when he shot one. I had to finish it off

There was something about hunting and the knowledge of hounds that appealed to. I was fascinated by the way hounds found the scent of a fox and stuck to it. magnificent thing. The great thing is patience. You cannot be impatient and Jack though he was a very exuberant sort of person was immensely patient with hounds. If you try to lead hounds they will let you and that is fatal when you are on foot in the mountains. The hounds must always hunt themselves because often they are far, far away.

I learned a lot from Jack. Not only about hunting. About the birds and the wild life. About the majestic silences and the mountains themselves. The weather and clouds which could suddenly clear to show you a precipice beneath your feet that you did not know was there.

It also kept me terribly fit. Sometimes I would end up on the side of Snowdon about four o'clock in the afternoon and I would have to walk back almost to Pwllheli, to Abererch, which would be about twenty miles. If you are fit and harden yourself when you are young it really does pay off in later life. The reason I am fit at eighty now is that when I was a boy I hunted in all weathers, trying to keep up with the hounds. As I walked I watched. I noted in my mind the shapes of clouds above me and below. I saw the sun bursting on to the grassy breasts of the hills as it broke through the clouds, creating glittering explosions of light that raced across the valleys and hills. The movements of the clouds as they swept over the mountains, dragging great shadows behind them, began to fascinate me and, as I watched, the knowledge that would later be useful to me as a painter I stored, sub consciously in my head.

When I did begin to paint it came second to hunting. Then one day in February 1947 hounds were meeting at Pen y Gwrydd. I had taken a couple of canvases with me and I started painting about nine o clock in the morning above Pen y Gwrydd and waited for the hounds to arrive. I could see them at the meet in the distance but I went on painting. In that moment I realised that creativity took preference over destruction. After that painting always took first place

In August later that year I was staying in a little pub called Gernant at the foot of Cader Idris. Although I had been at the Slade I did not know I was a painter really. I took two canvases and sketch books and climbed up to Llyn y Gadair, which is just under the summit, and painted an oil. I pegged it and with a canvas on my back I climbed up the Foxes Path to the top of Cader, went over the summit and did some drawings of Llyn

Cau on the other side. I came back to the top, down the Foxes Path and painted another picture at the bottom and pegged it again. Those were the first two paintings when I thought I might have a future as a painter. I don't know that I thought they were good but they were the first pictures I had ever painted that made me think I might be a painter and not a schoolmaster.

Roger Williams Evans recalls

Colonel Evan had died by the time I went there but four of the sisters still lived with Jack and another lived nearby in Llanystumdwy. She was considered very superior because she had been out to France as a governess and could speak French fluently.

In the house there was Minnie the public figure, the magistrate who called her car Jane Austen, Sybil who used to snap questions at you, Miggsie and poor little Annie who did all the chores. What little gossip they didn't know wasn't worth knowing.

The house was littered with fox skins, paws and masks. No electricity, just oil lamps.

The hunting country was mountainous but John was very fleet of foot. He had this ability to leap from rock to rock. You had to be tough to follow hounds at all. The weather was usually dreadful. Sleet you couldn't see through, or driving rain.

Didn't worry us. When we were hungry we would get behind a wall and eat a sandwich. Then from John's back pocket out would come a small pad. Rain or snow meant nothing. He drew whatever was in front of him whatever the weather.

The pack knew every inch of the mountains. Once they found their way into Llanfrothen church during a service. A church-warden crept to the pulpit where the parson was in mid sermon.

"The Ynysfor hounds is in the church," he whispered.

"Then show them to the Ynysfor pew," replied the cleric who had a fine sense of the obligation due to landed proprietors.

Minnie Jones always had an ear for a tale. It was she who told of visiting a tenant and hearing her call her dog forty different names, every one of which meant dungheap. She told Kyffin of a meeting with the water bailiff in Llanfrothen.

He said "Oh Miss Minnie. The other day I was in Cwm Croeso and I see something up the road. And I say to myself well damn is that a man or a bullock. And I look closer and duw it's neither. It's Mr Clough Williams-Ellis."

The house was a magnet to Kyffin. In summer after hunting was over he shot crows and pigeons, helped to bring in the hay and listened enraptured to the stories the family told as they sat in a semi circle round the drawing room fire.

Once, Captain Jack told him, he was swimming in the deep junction pool of the Glasfryn and the Ynysfor rivers where a police sergeant was searching for a farmer who had disappeared. Years later an elderly man called Hansen recently retired from the Indian police came to Kyffin for lessons in water colour painting. Over lunch he said he had been tracing his Danish ancestors among the Skagerrak and Kattegatt islands where they had lived. On one island where nearly everyone shared his name the harbour master sent for the only islander who spoke English. An English overlaid by a strong Welsh accent.

Though the two got on well it was only when Hansen was about to leave that very reluctantly the Welshman told his story.

> More than twenty years ago I was farming in the Glaslyn Valley in Caernarfonshire. One day Megan my wife came back from Porthmadog market with a bright yellow scarf in her basket. "Look Ifan," she said. "I've bought this to go to chapel on Sunday." Damn it, it was an awful thing so I told her straight "Megan, if you wear that thing for chapel I'll go away and never come back."
>
> Well you know what women are like. What does she do but go off to chapel the next Sunday with the scarf round her neck. Come the next Sunday and there she was going out of the house with the damn thing round her neck again. Defying me she was. A man must have his pride. I watched her till she went through the gate. Then I packed a bag and went to Porthmadog where a schooner was loading a cargo of slates. She brought me here and I am bloody not going back.

Another eager follower of the Ynysfor Hounds and one of the most remarkable men in Wales is Ernest Naish who at 88 still runs three farms at Cwm Pennant, Trawsfynydd and Anglesey. He was huntsman to the pack for most of the twelve years he followed it. He is man of many talents. When he joined the pre-war Navy he was a dagger man, the fast track naval elite. This enables him to claim the Naval record for going on courses. Ten years. Alas, the day he joined his first ship he went for a typhoid inoculation. was jabbed with a dirty needle and became seriously ill.

Back ashore, he commanded a trials party which inspected

submarines on maiden voyages. He was about to board one when he was taken ill again. The submarine was *HMS Thetis*. He says "My successor is buried in Holyhead. A very painful thought that is with me all the time."

Invalided out, Naish bought an Anglesey sheep farm and weaving mill, though he knew nothing about either trade. "I just asked my neighbour what to do next." Good neighbours, obviously. He became an international authority on sheep and wove tweed of such beauty it was taken up by fashion houses in London and Paris. The war intervened. When he came back, the tweed market had been wiped out by an eighty per cent purchase tax.

Fortunately he found a part-time job to boost his farm income. He set up and ran the Ty Croes Guided Missile Station at RAF Valley, commanding fifteen jet fighters and a staff of a hundred. In his spare time. He remembers it as great fun: "I would do the morning milking, then fly down to the Air Show at Farnborough, say. Then fly back in time for the evening milking."

The Air Ministry asked him to go to Woomera in Australia to report on a new pilotless plane. He barely had time to buy his second farm from a small advert in the *Guardian*: "Five hundred-acre farm on Cwm Pennant, with cottages and fine Victorian villa, built by wealthy father of quarry owner. £4,500." He only had time to look at it from the road. He bought it the same day.

The bard asks: "Oh Lord, why did you make Cwm Pennant so lovely and the life of a shepherd so short?" In the matter of age Naish has made a liar out the bard but agrees with the sentiment: "I am part of this farm," he says "just like the pigs and the sheep. This is the worst land in the Cwm, a foot of peat on rock. It is a hard place to make a living but my heart is here. In forty years I have only spent four nights away. That is why I have a hobby that keeps me at home."

The hobby is painting. Although self-taught he is acknowledged to be a very fine painter by the few people he has allowed to see his work. Perhaps his main claim to fame though is that he taught Kyffin to paint. Naish won't exhibit. He did once and has regretted it ever since.

Kyffin twisted my arm to take part in this touring exhibition sponsored by the Countryside Commission. I put four or five in. He valued them at £500 apiece and I thought, that's fine, they are safe, no-one will pay that. Blow me if I didn't sell two. I made a resolution never to do a silly thing like that again.

That was some years ago but you can tell it still hurt when he told me the story:

I am a non-profit-making water-colourist because, frankly, I don't need the money. I paint purely for my own pleasure. I get an idea by walking round the farm and looking at things, then I come back and ruin a lot of old envelopes sketching on them. I cannot start painting until the picture is complete in my head. I start in one corner and work across the paper. I don't know any of the rules. Never had a lesson. Don't know why I paint and why I paint such big pictures. It is very exacting. It takes hours and hours. My eyes and my limbs are going so I can only manage twenty minutes at a time.

This polymath has also designed a water-driven Aga in which an electric heater is powered from a generator he built which is fed from his stream and a machine which extracts heat from cold air. As he says, "Nothing really. Just reverse the principle of the fridge."

He has followed hounds for forty years. In 2000 he took a break from sheep shearing to talk about his long friendship with Kyffin:

I discovered the Ynysfor pack when I was nineteen. Captain Jack was a funny withdrawn sort of man. Gruff and surly with a huge handlebar moustache. When he saw I was obsessed with the way hounds work he took me under his wing. I was certainly obsessed. My brother who was also in the navy bought a motor bike in China for £2. He did it up and sold it to me for £8 and I often rode it all the way up from Plymouth for a day's hunting with the Ynysfor. Jack liked me for that. I also got on well with Minnie. She was the shining star amongst them, the one with personality. On the day of her death she was to have had a picnic with my family. We could not believe it when we were rung up to be told she had died over her breakfast.

She loved telling stories. We were talking about broken English and she said she had the greatest difficulty keeping a straight face when she asked a local person about a relative who had tuberculosis "Duw Miss Minnie," the person said. "We do be very worried. She's dropping fat."

I first met John when he was 12 and his mother brought him to a meet at Ynysfor. He was younger than me but we quickly discovered we shared this obsession with the way hounds were. From then on we were inseparable. He won a prize at school for art but he refused to take an art book. There was a book on the scenting of hounds which was an account of some very interesting work a man had done in this field. Quite rightly he insisted that was what he wanted. Lent me the book. Very interesting it was too

The Ynysfor didn't attract a large field. Usually there was Captain Jack, another naval chap Harry Glyn, Cedric Maby, John, Roger and me.

One day John invited me to the Royal Welch Fusiliers St David's Day dinner and to stay over with his family at Abererch. The next day was a Sunday and John suggested that we go out and I could show him how to paint. We duly went out, I pulled out my paper and paints and showed him how to do it. Fifty years later he acknowledged it in a speech at a dinner. He remembered that I had told him how colours change. Burnt Sienna and Ultramarine Blue mixed together make grey. That was the first lesson and he quoted it.

We shared one memorable moment. People say foxes are terrified of the hounds but I remember I was out with Kyffin on Garn Madryn on Lleyn. We saw two foxes coming up towards us, occasionally sitting and listening to the hounds in the next field. Not a bit worried. Completely in control of their environment.

Look here. There are only three things animals are interested in and they all begin with F. Feeding, fighting and I leave you to guess what the third f is. It certainly isn't fear.

The third surviving member of the companions of Ynysfor was Cedric Maby who was to have a distinguished career as a diplomat. He was captured by the Japanese and interned in Peking before being sent to Turkey where he became Vice Consul at the Embassy in Istanbul in 1942.

He was in Istanbul during the period that Cicero, the valet of of the Ambassador Sir Hughe Knatchbull-Hugesson, a German master spy, stole Britain's secrets from the Embassy safe. Secrets so important that the Germans did not believe them and paid

Cicero in counterfeit money.

In Peking Mabey became an authority on classical China. When he retired to Wales he translated a thousand years of Chinese poetry into Welsh which was published as *The Red Cockerel*. He and his wife, the daughter of the Swedish Ambassador to Turkey, were fervent Welsh Nationalists.

He recalled the pre-war Hunt Fortnight of the Anglesey Harriers. Hunting every day and dining and dancing in the Bulkeley Hotel at Beaumaris every evening. It was from this energetic orgy that the custom began which still thrives of throwing shovelfuls of hot pennies to the crowds in the streets.

Recalled Cedric:

> Ynysfor hangers-on wanted to know why we couldn't have a ball like the people in Anglesey. Captain Jack was against it and regular followers agreed with him. But Colonel Evan seized every opportunity to wear the dashing hunt uniform with its red tail coat and blue facings so a Ball was planned.
>
> We booked the Oakley Arms at Maentwrog which has the most elegant ballroom and applied to the magistrates for an extension. To our amazement it was turned down. Minnie was furious. She was a magistrate too, of course. She got into Jane Austen and drove off to give the licensing magistrate the rough edge of her tongue. He was terribly apologetic. "Oh Miss Minnie," he said. "I didn't realise they was Church hounds. I thought they was Chapel hounds. That's why I turned them down.
>
> The decision was reversed but the magistrate was taking no chances. As closing time approached the village policeman arrived on his bicycle. Captain Jack didn't really approve of balls and he had spent most of the evening in the public bar with his cronies.
>
> He spotted the policeman and offered him a drink. I have two memories of that ball. Minnie and Clough Williams-Ellis opening the ball with the most spirited Viennese waltz you have ever seen and the policeman riding his bicycle in circles o20, n the Oakley car park with an expression on his face of utter bliss.

Kyffin remembers the ball. His partner was the granddaughter of Lloyd George. "I was obsessed with the girl. I was terribly susceptible as a young man." He admitted that at 80 he still was.

Captain Jack was to die tragically in 1948 whilst hunting his hounds. A fox went to ground in a rocky earth above the bridge at Penmaen Pool near Dolgellau. A farmer warned him the rocks were unsafe but Jack ignored him. Seconds later he was pinned under falling rocks and killed. The estate and the hounds passed to a soldier nephew, Edmund Roache, a difficult, sulky man. In the bad winter of 1974 when even the tractors were frozen, Roache had a row with his kennelman Robert about a job that had not been done. Robert said he would have done it if he hadn't to spend so much time with the hounds. In a fit of anger Roache stormed off to the kennels and shot twelve hounds. The young entry he gave away. It was the end of the Ynysfor Hunt

The Eryri Hounds, with whom Kyffin still hunted regularly until his death, were founded by a neighbouring landowner and friend of Edmund Roache, Prys Williams of Hafod-y-Llan. Prys's family had been tenant farmers on the Hafod-y-llan and Gelli Iago estates at Nant Gwynant since the seventeenth century. The estates comprise a third of Yr Wyddfa (Snowdon) and include the peaks of Snowdon, Lliwedd and Cnicht. Prys bought them and in a stroke became the biggest and most powerful landowner in the mountains. Williams and Roache were hunting in the Lake District when Roache was offered two couple of hounds by the Windermere Foot Harriers. He turned them down because they were too small. Williams took them to hunt hare on another farm he owned on Anglesey. Then he started hunting foxes in the Ynysfor country. This made Roache furious. He abandoned the slopes of Snowdon which Williams owned and farmed and the two men never spoke again. Occasionally the two hunts met. On such occasions Roache left his hounds with Naish to bring home and drove off in his Landrover with darkened brow.

Williams's estate included the ruins of Brynkir Hall. In the early part of the nineteenth century Brynkir had been bought by a family named Huddard. They were a kindly family, Kyffin remembered:

> They found work for unemployed tenants building roads and cottages on the estate. Indeed it became a family tradition that when an heir inherited he got local men to build another room onto their house. Presumably from the same charitable motives

the family also built Brynkir tower, a wonderful folly on a hill, ideal for a Rapunzel to let down her hair and recently restored by Prys's grandson, the present master of the hounds, Richard Williams and his wife Frances a descendant of Beatrix Potter.

The Huddard estate came up for sale when a gambling Huddard lost all the family money. It is said he was so obsessed he would bet on two snails racing across a chessboard. Things became so bad and the creditors so demanding that one morning he and his family vanished, leaving the breakfast things unwashed on the table and the house gradually fell into ruin.

Wendy Wynn Williams was one of the few girls allowed to follow the Ynysfor Hounds. Her ancestors were Williams Wynn until one of them started a money lending business in Chester which became Williams Bank and then with an Anglesey man started the vast Dorothea Quarry. He changed his name because he thought himself grander than the Williams Wynns.

The quarry owners were hard task masters. At the time of the Irish Potato Famine starving Irish families came over looking for work. Her great grandfather would only employ them if they changed their religion and became non-conformists. A lot of the workers were related to the family. She said "I remember walking round with my grandfather and people saying 'Morning cousin'. My grandmother snootily referred to them as 'Welsh cousins'."

> The workers were not badly paid. Many of them invested in the shipping firms the quarries owned. They all had a plot of land, a cow, chickens and a pig, a small holding the wife ran.
>
> But they were only paid when they could work. No pay if they were rained off. There is an eight mile wall round the Vaynol Estate. No wages for the local men who built it. They were paid in bags of corn.

At 74, and married to Lt Col Roy Davies, a fellow subaltern of Kyffin's in the Royal Welch Fusiliers, she recalled there were conditions.

> I was not allowed to speak. Captain Jack hated chatter. Very few girls went out. I was honoured but I had to be like a boy. No rubbish like being helped over a style. Ten mile points.
>
> I remember the teenaged John Kyffin, terribly thin and

spindly, pale complexion and huge ears sticking out. He looked like a silver birch. He was a terribly nice boy with a terrific sense of humour. But terribly shy He was a special favourite with the Ynysfor. All the other boys were 'That Boy'. He was the only one Captain Jack called by his name.

After hunting we would troop back to Ynysfor for a boiled egg tea. Followers had an egg each. Only John was a two egg man. An honour he shared with Colonel Evan and Captain Jack. The family loved him. They reckoned his mother didn't look after him.

To help Kyffin they commissioned him to paint Captain Jack's portrait. Everyone was very keen except Captain Jack. He made Kyffin muck out three huts before he would sit for him. The portrait is still at Ynysfor, though I have never seen it exhibited.

The Ynysfors were out of this world. They belonged to old Wales. They still carried on the ancient tradition of Welsh hospitality. Any house of any distinction kept open house. My grandfather remembered there was always a pan of cawl on the kitchen fire. Any traveller who called was given a bowl.

Kyffin remembered their mother who kept to the old way of eating. The main meal of the day was at lunchtime and in the evening she had only a bowl of buttermilk. Even when they had smart dinner parties old Mrs Jones would insist on her bowl of *bara minim*.

The hounds were not over fed. There was one story you never dared repeat in front of the Captain. A kennel huntsman must have gone into the hounds late one night. In the morning all that was left of him was his boots.

Of the Miss Joneses, Minnie was the worldly one. She had been to America to show the Americans how to hunt foxes. She had several boyfriends. One who doted on her was a local curate who came to tea on a hot day. He sat down at the table and said "I sweat something awful". That was the end of him.

They were a great power in the land and it did not do to cross them. The bench in Porthmadog consisted of Colonel Evan, Captain Jack and Miss Minnie. A lady of ill repute was giving evidence. Miss Minnie said "She's guilty" and couldn't be persuaded she was only a witness and could not be punished. They had somebody who was a terrible poacher. No question of a court appearance for him. Colonel Evan and Captain Jack caught him and threw him in the river.

Miss Sybil wore flighty hats. She would appear at a tea party in a bright pink hat with a veil whereas the other sisters wore sensible woolly hats.

Miss Miggs was the homely one who boiled the eggs. They

had little maids from the village who were terrified of anyone who spoke English. They were frightened of taking stuff into the dining room, they used to try to get me to take it in for them.

Captain Jack was larger than life. I remember once I was sitting on the bonnet of a Lagonda car and we drove into Llanfrothen with some boys inside and others hanging on the running board. There was a pub in Llanfrothen and, as we passed, out through the window came a man. It was Captain Jack, moustache bristling "What are you doing with that scum. Get back home girl."

Staying at Ynysfor was quite an experience. It was lit by oil lamps. Dark brown paintwork and hanging over the banisters was a huge rug of foxskin with masks all round the house. It was a jewel. You had all these other families around which were new money. The Ynysfors weren't. They were only slightly anglicised. They all spoke Welsh on the hearth

I wasn't old enough to go to the Hunt Ball but there was a terrible to-do. You daren't mention it to Captain Jack. He insisted I wasn't to go.

It was Great Aunt Cecily who first named Colonel Evan Jones Sentimental Evan. She almost got him into terrible trouble. The Anglesey Hunt Fortnight was a great time. There had been a real steeple chase; literally from steeple to steeple. That ended when two people were killed. The Anglesey Hunt Ball was the great climax. It was held in the old Bulkeley Assembly Rooms which had a balcony round the ballroom. Great Aunt Cecily was up on the balcony and Colonel Evan was below with his arm round a girl. Cecily dropped a piece of ice cream down this girl's front and she screamed her head off. Everyone thought Colonel Evan had done something he shouldn't. But Lady Bulkeley had seen what happened and told on her.

Another girl who was an occasional follower was Kyffin's only living blood relation, his cousin Betty Mewies. She would come every year from her home in Stretford, Lancashire, for a fortnight's holiday with the Williamses at Plas Gwyn, near Criccieth. She told me:

> I met John Kyffin and his brother Dick for the first time when I was twelve and fell passionately in love with them both. I think there is nothing unusual in that. There is a great affinity with first cousins and besides they were both in their different ways so eminently lovable. Dick was the more glamorous, he was tall and darkly handsome; he smoked Passing Cloud and wore a cravat.

John Kyffin was small and frail. He was known as Little John. He showed me great instinctive kindness. It was unusual because he was fifteen and at that age boys do not want girls of twelve hanging round. He used to take me out walking and taught me a lot about birds. He would shoot rabbits but he loved birds. I remember once he rescued a small owl with a broken wing and he was so gentle. He carried it home and nursed it back to health in a games room at the rear of the house. I say I loved him. I should have said everyone loved him. Even my mother who found fault with everyone could find none in Kyffin.

We used to holiday in Anglesey. We would all be on the beach. Dick and Little John used to swim. Dick, a big strong lad, used to come out of the water and Aunt Essylt, his mother used to wrap him in a huge towel and rub him briskly the minute he stepped on dry land. When Little John came out of the water he was ignored and that sums up the way their family worked. Dick was never allowed to clear a table or wash up; little John and I had to.

There was another side of John Kyffin which he keeps very quiet about. His music. He cannot read a note but we used to go to the pictures at Porthmadog. If it was a musical he would come and sit at the piano. And play the pieces note perfect. Dick had lessons but Kyffin played entirely by ear.

Aunt Essylt, who was one of the first women drivers, used to take us to the meet at Ynysfor in her car. One day smoke began to pour out of the engine. It was me who had to go to a nearby farm for a bucket of water whilst the boys sat in the car.

We used to hunt in all sorts of weather. I had mixed feelings about hunting. When the fox passed me I didn't always tell anyone and I hated it when the fox went to ground and the terriers were sent in. But the farmers insisted on it. Ynysfor wasn't a recreation. It was a pest exterminator.

TWO

The Byzantine complexities of Kyffin's pedigree were unravelled in his autobiography *Across the Straits,* a minor classic and an account of a Welsh world now lost. When it was first published in 1973 the book caused a furore among the deeply class-conscious Gwynedd society whose antics it recorded with great glee. *Across the Straits* was republished in 1998 so it is necessary only to summarise an ancestry that sometimes seems more a library of plots for scandalous historical novels than a family tree. A tree which includes King Philip of France and, via his daughter, Edward I, who conquered Wales with an army of 15,000 which included 9,000 South Walians. Kyffin also descends from Edward II's favourite Sir Hywel y Pedolau (Howell of the Horseshoes), the giant son of the king's nurse who flamboyantly broke horseshoes in battle to discomfort enemies.

The first recorded non-giant, non-royal male ancestor, in 1666, was Wmffre ap William John ap Rhys, who came from yeoman stock and was village blacksmith in the Anglesey hamlet of Llansadwrn. According to a local legend, he had tethered a difficult horse to a tree stump outside his smithy. The horse pulled out the stump and beneath its roots ap Rhys found a pot of gold. The truth was rather more prosaic. When he was twenty Wmffre married Catherine Meredydd, an eighty-eight year old heiress. With her dowry he bought a farm, endowed alms houses, instituted charities and anglicised his name to Humphrey Williams. His family were the issue of a second wife Margaret Prydderch. His son Owen bought Treffos, the manor house of the parish where the family was to live until a descendant sold it a hundred and fifty years later in 1904.

A roadman told Kyffin the story of one young Mr Williams of

Treffos and the snake:

> They sent him away to school in England and he came home
> with a snake. And an old woman in the village said if Mr Williams
> keeps that snake he is dead just like that. Well what did they do?
> They sent him to South Africa. Years later young Mr Williams
> came back from South Africa. He was walking across the field in
> front of the house. And he tread on this thing in the ground and
> something went into his foot. And do you know what it was ? It
> was the skeleton of the snake. And the bone went into young Mr
> Williams' foot and he got blood poisoning and dead, just like
> that. The old woman was right.

Treffos was famous as many Anglesey gardens are for its rhododendrons. On a bus once going past the house Kyffin heard two old women talking: "Oh look at those lovely hydenrons," said one. The other said, "Don't be so silly they are not hydenrons. They are rhodydandoms."

Owen had two sons. One, John, became Chaplain to Princess Augusta of Wales and held three livings on Anglesey. In the ancient courtroom of the nearby town of Beaumaris there is a plaster cast in the magistrates retiring room. It shows a farmer tugging the tail of a cow and another its horns whilst, sitting at his ease, a solicitor milks it. A visual description of the career of Owen's other son Thomas who bought the family's second Anglesey manor Craig y Don.

A country solicitor he managed to represent both sides in a dispute over the ownership of the mineral rights of Parys Mountain, one of the most valuable copper sites in Britain. By the time it was settled in 1785 Thomas controlled the mine whilst his clients had become sleeping partners. He produced his own coinage, two hundred and fifty tons of pennies and 50 tons of halfpences, some designed by a Coventry jeweller Francis Skidmore. This money which the miners could spend in company stores shows a druid's head encircled by a wreath bearing twenty-four acorns, the Parys Mountain company logo and the legend 'Success to the Anglesey Miners'. Thomas hoped the issue would lead to a contract to produce British Crown coinage. It did not, largely because he fell out with Prime Minister Pitt. But he controlled the whole of the British copper industry, becoming in the process a millionaire, an MP and founder of the Williams Chester and North Wales Bank. This became the nucleus of the Midland and the vast industrial empire he built, the nucleus of ICI. Yet he was not the archetypal capitalist grinding the faces of the poor. His nickname amongst his miners was 'Tom Chwarae Teg', Tom Fair Play.

Thomas's descendants mainly concerned themselves with spending rather than making fortunes. One grandson Owen commanded the Royal Horse Guards. The other, Hwfa, built Sandown Park race course and became a director of the Savoy, Claridges, the Berkeley and Simpsons in the Strand.

Through Owen, the brothers and their six beautiful sisters had the entree to the Marlborough House set over which the future Edward VII genially presided. As a result, all the sisters, including Edith the most wayward, found aristocratic husbands. Edith who drove a four in hand of ostriches became one of the legion of Edward's mistresses whilst dallying with the Marquess of Blandford. This caused both the Prince of Wales and Hwfa to challenge the Marquess to a duel. On neither occasion was a shot fired but Hwfa was subsequently injured in the leg when a demented post office clerk wildly fired a revolver at him in The Mall.

Marriage caused much greater damage. Hwfa's bride was a fortune hunter Florence Farquharson who moved to Paris after he died and succeed in spending his last penny a few days before her own death. She wrote a book called *It Was Such Fun*. That title and Queen Victoria's remark "The Williamses are a bad family" seem to sum up that branch of the family.

Meanwhile the Royal Chaplain Owen's branch of the family, from which Kyffin Williams descends, were irredeemably good. It continued to pour out a succession of worthy clergymen, twenty-seven in all: Every one country parsons who over two hundred years occupied nearly every living on the north western coast of Anglesey. His family is also connected to Sir William Vincent of Bangor who in the 1920's was the Permanent Head of the Indian Civil Service, represented India at the League of Nations and was the architect of the continent's Independence in 1948.

His great grandmother Frances was a painter who charted the

Menai Straits as a teenager. Her husband James's parish, Llanfairynghornwy on Anglesey, had a coastline of dangerous reefs where ships were frequently wrecked. On March 26 1823, the day they came back from their honeymoon, a packet boat *The Alert* struck West Mouse rock and broke up. Out of 140 people on board there were only seven survivors. They could only watch in horror as the others drowned. There had no boat sufficiently well found to broach the angry seas.

James and Frances determined to buy one. He dunned the local gentry for subscriptions. She made lithographs of a painting she had done when George IV made his only visit to Anglesey. Their Anglesey Lifeboat Service was founded before the RNLI which took it over in 1856. The rescue boat was based at Cemlyn Bay below his rectory. James coxed it and Frances often joined his crew of farmers to nurse injured survivors. Together they saved 400 lives and James won the first RNLI gold medal for bravery to come to Wales. Ironically he won it not in the boat but on horseback. On March 7 1835 the *SS Active*, a Belfast cargo boat was wrecked in breakers so high the rescue boat could not be launched. James leaped on his horse and swam it out to sea to throw a grappling iron in to the *Active's* bowsprit rigging, saving the crew of five.

If Kyffin Williams inherited his painting gifts from his great grandmother his impish sense of humour comes from her son, his grandfather Owen, a country clergyman and like his father a Chancellor of Bangor Cathedral, incidentally the highest office the family achieved. A parishioner of Kyffin's grandfather told him: "He was telling me of the time when he was hit in the eye by a ball at school. How they was to take him to hospital, take his eye out and put it on a plate in front of him and how he was see as well with his eye on the plate as he could with it in his head."

Owen was infected with his parents' passion for lifeboats. His first parish Bodfuan was in the centre of the Lleyn Peninsula which enabled him to cox lifeboats on both coasts.

One of his relatives recalled how she was being driven by Owen in a gig. At the foot of the hill on which the rectory stood the pony halted and refused to budge. "Maggie Jones," called Owen. "Send out the pig." The cottage door opened and out shot

a small pig which bolted up the hill closely followed d by the pony.
Two of the parson's sons, James and John – Betty Mewies's
father, went to sea and fought for revolutionaries in Chile:

> John, who was always known in the village as Mr Johnny, was
> small and freckled and totally without fear. If ever a horse had to
> be broken they sent for Mr Johnny. He went out with my Uncle
> James to Chile in 1880 to fight for the revolutionaries against
> Spain. James stayed out there and became a Captain in the
> Chilean navy.

John came back married to an awful woman, the daughter of a
Antwerp harbour master: "Josephine," said Kyffin, "who was all
sorts of hell wrapped up". He sent a joking word to the rectory
that he was coming back with his bride and she was foreign. To
the locals that meant she was black. The word got out. Mr Johnny
has married a black woman. He was a popular figure. Kyffin tells
the story:

> I once went to see an old lady in Llanfairynghornwy. She was
> about 90 and I had never seen her before. To my astonishment
> she got up and threw her arms about me kissing me passionately.
> I realised she thought I was Uncle John. He had gone to sea and
> used to put in at Liverpool where she was in service.

And Betty Mewies recalls:

> Later my great nephew found out that to this day he is venerated
> by the Chileans. He was a very adventurous person. John Kyffin
> loved him. Kyffin looks exactly like his father, Harry, another of
> the brothers. They were both very gentle, unlike my father.

Kyffin was very aware of his family and his position in it: "My
family lost all its money and ceased to be county. I am the end of
the line. The inverted peak of a very large triangle. I have illegitimate relations on Anglesey but I am sworn to secrecy."

His great uncle Tom Kyffin was rector of Llanbadrig, of which
the patron was Lord Stanley of Alderley, a Mohammedan.
Through the Bishop of Bangor, the Rev Tom asked Stanley to
restore the church, and another at nearby Bodewryd. He agreed
provided they were restored in an Islamic manner. There is
abstract glass and Islamic tiles behind the altar.

This Lord Stanley bred labradors and two of Kyffin's needy aunts, Annia and Mamie, heard that if anyone praised the colour of his golden retrievers he would always say; "Do you really think it a lovely colour? May I give you a length of tweed in the same colour?" It worked for the aunts too.

His funeral was bizarre. He was succeeded by a Roman Catholic priest. As the coffin was lowered the new Lord Stanley took off his top hat. Only to be kicked by his brother. "Not your hat, you bloody fool. Its your shoes you remove." This later Lord Stanley was reputed to have a Spanish gypsy mistress whom he kept in Elen's Tower on the cliffs at South Stack.

Kyffin's uncle, Guy Williams, had an exotic connection. He was a general in charge of recruiting in the Far East. On a visit to Tonga he threw a party for Queen Salote's husband who became so drunk he keeled over and died. Uncle Guy had to break the news to the Queen. He insisted that telling the Queen he had killed the king: it was the bravest thing he had done.

Kyffin's great grandfather was impressed by a poor boy who was a teacher at Rhosybol. He got my mother's grandfather to teach him Greek and Latin and eventually got him into Jesus, Oxford. His name was John Rhys and he became the first Professor of Celtic Studies and Principal of Jesus and was the man who said famously when a suggestion was mooted there should be baths at Jesus: "What, may I ask you, is the point? They are only up here for eight weeks."

A third son Harry, Kyffin's father, was considered too delicate to work, indeed he only went to school briefly in Southport. He became a wood carver until he decided to make a career in banking about which he knew nothing. He joined the North and South Wales Bank which had taken over the family operation. He was given a revolver and a terrier and told to open a branch at Penydarren in the then lawless Rhondda.

Harry Williams was a tall, handsome man with a nature so lovable that the locals took to him at once. He was the antithesis of the traditional bank manager. He trusted everyone. He played the organ in the church and as a gesture of appreciation to the people of Penydarren he carved a lovely reredos over the altar.

From the Rhondda he moved as a clerk to Midland Bank

branches in PortHmadog, Caernarfon and finally to Llangefni back home on the Isle of Anglesey.

Late in life he married Essylt Mary, the daughter of another vicar from the adjoining parish. Where Harry was outgoing she was withdrawn. Her mother had been a chronic invalid, prey to migraine attacks and had spent much of her life in a dark room, her head swathed in brown paper. After her mother's death Essylt's girlhood was spent with her gloomy father whom she worshiped. When she was sent to bed she would creep out onto the landing to look at him adoringly, as he smoked unaware below. He seems incapable of feeling. His diary entry for 1st July 1883 reads "Showery. Little girl born at 12.30 pm."

He sent the desperately insecure small girl to boarding school in London, where she was so lonely she ran away and thereafter was educated by a stream of governesses, who served only to repress her further. Unwillingly, and paralysed with shyness, she played hostess at parish teas. At one, a farmer told an improper story which gave her the unshakeable view that Welshmen were vulgar. She forbade anyone ever after to speak Welsh in her presence. Her revulsion to the language extended to her name. In Welsh form it is Essylt. Her father gave her the name because he was reading about Essylt in the *Mabinogion* when she was born. It was a name she hated but her father insisted that if she weren't to be known by her Welsh name he would call her Polly which she thought vulgar

Although related to leading Anglesey families she was treated as a poor relation by them. Her relatives the Rice Roberts lived in some state in a fine house called Rhiwlas nut the children were never allowed to visit Essylt at her rectory home which their mother considered low. At family dances she was never allowed to sleep in the big house. A bed was found in a nearby cottage.

By the time of her marriage at the age of thirty-four, Essylt was a mass of inhibitions. In the mechanics of marriage and mother-hood she excelled. She was a fine cook and a careful house-keeper. She was desperate to do the right thing yet incapable of showing affection. Kyffin, the youngest son, cannot remember ever being kissed or cuddled by her. Never having known love she was incapable of showing it. As though she

realised this, she attempted to make up by being over protective
of her two sons, especially Richard. Forty years later Kyffin
suggested that Richard by now ill and the frail bubble of his self
esteem irrevocably punctured should take a holiday abroad. His
mother was horrified. A trip abroad. his first, would have put him
beyond her protection. It did not happen. He said:

> My mother suffered from a very deep inferiority complex. When
> we inherited the house on Anglesey we were ostracised. Her
> cousin, who was disinherited, was part of the hunting set on
> Anglesey and all the hunting people took her side against my
> mother. They were utterly beastly to my mother. They refused to
> call on her at all.
>
> One of them, Claire Daniel, who used to push me in my pram
> when I was a baby came up to me when I talked about the
> ostracism in my book. She said "You were quite right to mention
> it. I am totally ashamed of myself." In contrast my father got on
> with everyone. Although my mother was emotional she never
> showed it. She never showed any interest in my painting. When I
> had my first exhibition in London in 1948 she came up, saw it
> but was not impressed. She would never compliment me. She
> went round it without saying a word. She couldn't show her
> feeling when my father died in 1941 she didn't seem to be
> concerned at all.

Wendy Davies thought of her as fey. "She was not a caring
mother the Ynysfor family thought she did not feed Kyffin, which
is why he always got two eggs I suppose."

Ernie Naish remembers Essylt: "She was an odd woman. She
didn't want to be a Welsh person; she wanted to be English and
look down on the Welsh. His father was the reverse. He was never
happier than when he was nattering away in Welsh. She was small
and unimpressive. Very correct and standoffish. Never happier
than when she was talking about the old landed families of
Anglesey. Though I must say she was always very decent to me."

Roger Williams Evans agrees: "His father was jovial but I
always found his mother depressing. She never understood why
he wanted to paint and never had a good word for him. She
concentrated on Dick who had a very unhappy life. He wasn't
allowed to marry the girl he wanted. Her parents were against the
match."

Betty Mewies had happier memories:

> Aunt Essylt was very, very kind to me I must say. I think she was
> a woman born before her time. She was a very clever woman,
> deeply frustrated. Had she gone to University there was no
> telling what she might have accomplished.
>
> She was a very efficient woman. A wonderful organiser. I
> remember she used to give coffee mornings for the church, long
> before anyone had heard of coffee mornings. She started the
> Hospital Linen Fund where people gave a penny a week to
> provide blankets for the local cottage hospital. I have always
> understood that Aunt Essylt's linen fund was the precursor of the
> Hospital Saturday Fund with its penny a week subscription.
>
> She was a stickler for etiquette, I remember. She told me that
> it was wrong at a dinner to wait for the hostess before you begin
> to eat. No hostess wants her guests to let their dinners go cold.

It was always Kyffin, never Richard, who did the family chores.
It might be supposed that this favouritism would have affected the
brothers' relationship. Not so. "He was always so sweet, so loving
and so kind," Kyffin recalled. "I knew I was the second child and
my brother was number one. He was brilliant at everything. I
knew he was better than I was so I was never jealous. I couldn't
resent him because from the moment I became conscious I knew
he was better. I was told so by my mother but it was unarguable.
When I scrambled my way into Shrewsbury he was a bit of a
swell. In both cricket and soccer teams. He was terribly, terribly
good to me. We got on extremely well. I remember once I hit him
because he wouldn't play with me. All he did was look at me with
his large eyes and I felt an absolute shit. He was extremely kind
but hopelessly over sensitive."

Later it was Kyffin who was the dominant brother, as Richard
slipped into alcoholism and obsessive gambling. Outwardly he did
well. At school he was captain of school rugby, a first class
footballer and cricketer, excelled at fives, running, Richard was
house monitor, top of the Modern Side. All boys in the Modern
Sixth got an automatic scholarship to Oxbridge.

Kyffin told me "I didn't know of his tragedy for thirty years
and then he told me":

> Shrewsbury had a system of fagging called dowling, from *dowlos*
> the Greek for slave. Until boys had been at the school for two

years they were called dowls. If a monitor wanted something
doing he opened his study door and shouted "Dowl". The last
boy did the dirty work. Dick thought he hear a shout and ran to
a monitor's door. The monitor said "What do you want funny
face?" That was the moment my brother's life was destroyed.
Something hit him hard. After a year he thought he had a very
funny face, after two years he believed he was so repulsive no-
one wanted to look at him. He was very good looking but it so
affected him he could not function. He couldn't ask for rooms
anywhere. If the landlady said she was full up he believed the real
reason was because he was so repulsive. I had to look for rooms
for him. If someone crossed the street it was because they did not
want to look at his face. It's a known medical condition, I believe.

He refused to take an Oxford scholarship. Our school reports
are with the Bangor archivist. You can see the masters were
puzzled by Dick. He did go to Jesus College but not on a scholarship. He did no work at all. He spent his whole time in sport
and idled his way through a course in Modern Languages. He
was to go into the Indian Civil Service but he only managed a
third. He went into a solicitor's office in Pwllheli until the war. He
joined the Royal Welch as a private soldier. I was an officer and
we used to have clandestine meetings. He later got a commission
but it was another tragedy. He was sent on a battle school course.
The instructors were throwing plastic hand grenades. One
landed in a gorse bush and blew his leg off. It didn't worry him
all that much because he knew he was revolting. This was merely
underlining it. Not only was his face revolting, he only had one
leg. I had to tell my mother and I do not think she ever got over
it.

After the war Dick worked as a solicitor for Walker, Smith and
Way in Chester where he was much loved by everyone who knew
him, including this biographer. His erudition and fusillades of
Latin tags demolished many a prosecutor. Affable enough, but
one always felt he had built a wall round himself it would have
been impossible to breach. It was heart rending to see his lonely
figure stumping into the magistrates' court in the Town Hall.
Eventually he retired to Anglesey where Kyffin protected him
from everything but the spectres in his own mind until he gave up
the struggle and died.

Recalled Kyffin,

Twice I think he tried to kill himself. When he was forty he went to live in an old folks' home. When it closed a colleague Dennis Diamond found him rooms in a pub in Rossett, He became an alcoholic and took an overdose of pills but he recovered.

Dennis found him more rooms but he was getting more and more depressed and every night he went to bed hoping he wouldn't wake up.

He came back to Anglesey but things went from bad to worse. One day I gave him a lift to Beaumaris. He said in a very firm voice "Goodbye". The next day his landlady rang to tell me he had been found dead.

Despite his twenty-seven family clerics Kyffin was always a non-believer, though he had one thing in common with them. They were never happier than when talking about the oddities of their flock to whom they were tireless visitors. Kyffin's 'parish' included old family retainers like Nanny Williams, Fingar, so called because she lived in Llansadwrn near the signpost. A tough little body and a passionate supporter of Manchester United, she preferred being called Nanny Williams Verney. She was a terrible snob and that was the name of the baronet she worked for. She was horrified when her sister died and was buried on the side of the church path where the ordinary people went and not on the other side with the Pobl Mawr.

Once when Kyffin visited her he was startled to be asked; "Do you ever see that Kyffin Williams fellow?"

He said he did. Why?

"Will you give him a message from me? Will you say him damn and blast?"

"What for?" he asked

"Because he never comes to see me."

Kyffin had more reason to feel neglected that Nanny Fingar. When he was born on Ascension Day 1918 in Tanygraig a small house on the outskirts of Llangefni on Anglesey his mother immediately put him out to be fostered by a neighbouring farmer's wife. He was only brought back to Tanygraig to attend his christening. Performed in a local church by his eighty-seven year old grandfather, who two years earlier had christened brother Richard. The only services he ever performed in English, presumably out of deference to his daughter in law.

Promotion took the family to Chirk where Harry Williams

became manager of the Midland Bank. There the boys had a succession of nurses, who were warned if they ever spoke Welsh they would be instantly dismissed. One had a more terrible gift to impart. All his life Kyffin believed that it was her cruelty which gave him epilepsy.

Outward appearances were more important in the Williams family than inner torment. Kyffin's father had always limped. The family were told that this was the result of an accident. His nurse had been taking him out in the pram when a herd of horses rushed by and knocked the pram into a ditch. Harry, it was said, broke his leg but the nurse was so frightened of admitting he had been in an accident she told no one and the leg healed itself awry.

Kyffin told the story in *Across the Straits*. Amongst his readers was the Chief Surgeon of the Orthopedic Hospital in Oswestry, founded incidentally by a Williams' cousin Agnes Hunt. He subsequently visited Kyffin at his home in Pwllfanogl on the Menai Strait and asked him to imitate the way his father walked. Kyffin did. "As I suspected," the surgeon said. "It's all rubbish about your father having an accident. He had a congenital abnormality of his hip. It was supposed when he was young to be disgraceful and a dishonour to the family. Obviously a story was made up to account for it."

Three years after he was appointed to Chirk Harry Williams broke his other leg in a fall, his health deteriorated and he retired. By this time Essylt had inherited Brynhyfryd a furnished house near Beaumaris in its own landscaped grounds. Unfortunately the aunt, Letty Pritchard, who left it left nothing to her already wealthy daughter. The daughter, Mary Pritchard Rayner, went to law and although the judge decided in the Williams' favour he ruled that each side should pay its own costs. The sum involved was well beyond the Williamses' means. The house was sold and the family moved to a rented home in South Caernarfonshire.

Wendy Davies believes the issue was a famous Rockingham tea service which was much prized in the family. "Lawsuits are definitely a pastime on Anglesey and Mary Pritchard Rayner sued them for the tea service. It would have been more sensible to have given her the tea service but Mrs Williams chose to defend and lost everything. Anglesey is very cliquey and ostracism was complete. She was not a very balanced person and that must have had a terrible effect on her."

There is perhaps a further more bizarre explanation of his mother's hurt. Coyly to some, more explicitly to others, Kyffin would say he was the natural son of his mother's contemporary Sir Richard Williams-Bulkeley. An elderly local journalist claims that in his youth he had been told the story of Mrs Williams' mesalliance. Kyffin himself admitted it to this biographer. What was puzzling was the physical resemblance of Kyffin to his mother's husband.

★ ★ ★

The Williams' new home was an ugly castellated house near the north eastern shores of Cardigan Bay, now a hotel. It is surrounded by the most glorious landscapes in Britain. As Kyffin wrote: "It was here I began to assemble unknowingly a vast library of feelings, sensations and knowledge that were to form the foundations of my future life as a landscape painter."

With the move to South Caernarfonshire began what Kyffin insisted was the happiest time of his life. He and his brother were sent to board at Tre-Arddur House school, a forbidding collection of buildings on a rocky hill above the beach on Holy Island, joined to Anglesey by a causeway and a bridge. Iorwerth Owen Williams the owner was a small dark vivid man from an old Anglesey family married to a kindly English woman. There was a wonderful atmosphere at the school where Kyffin spent his seventh birthday.

The master who taught Kyffin art at Tre-Arddur was F.H. Glazebrook a remarkable and inspirational man who lived for a while in a tent on Llandwyn beach and wrote the definitive guide book to Anglesey and the North Wales coast. He was a superb sailor and charted and published *Pilotage of the Menai Strait*. It was Glazebrook, a master of perspective who crystallised Kyffin's lifelong devotion to drawing as the basis of all visual art. It was here he won his first prize. Not for painting but for poetry. He was in quarantine with chicken pox. The pupils were asked to write a poem on the snow outside. His was judged the best.

As so often in Kyffin's life disaster was waiting in the wings. In

1929 he and Richard had their tonsils taken out. Richard recovered quickly but Kyffin was far from well. In the middle of his operation the surgeon had a heart attack, during which in a frenzied sweep of his scalpel he not only removed Kyffin's tonsils and adenoids, he took out the uvula and soft palate as well.

The family were not told of the accident. The hospital blamed his slow recovery on natural frailty. His parent found the truth in the oddest way. It was the custom in those days for a relation of a patient to call on the surgeon's wife. Kyffin's aunt Mamie called. In order to get to the front door of the surgeon's home in Upper Bangor she had to go through the conservatory where she saw a pair of boots among the geraniums. It was the surgeon. A second heart attack had killed him. Poor Aunt Mamie had to go to the door and when the surgeon's wife answered it say "I am frightfully sorry but your husband is dead amongst the geraniums."

Before the operation Kyffin had been a bright pupil and was being groomed as a future head of school. Afterwards he was unable to concentrate. Brother Richard easily won his scholarship to Shrewsbury. Not only was there no question of Kyffin achieving this, there were doubts he would even pass his Common Entrance examination. Friends tried to help. He was doing the algebra paper with the Vicar of Holyhead, the Rev Rowlands, as invigilator. "Having trouble, my boy?" the Vicar asked. "Let's go through it together." The Vicar did the whole paper. When the results came Kyffin had passed in every subject except algebra.

When he got to Shrewsbury School – the smallest boy there – he discovered that the boys who did best in examinations sat at the back of the class. Kyffin sat at the front. It was sometime before he realised they sat there because cheating was easier. Kyffin with his Welsh church upbringing could not bring himself to be dishonest. All the way through the lower school he was in consequence given up by his masters as hopeless.

Eventually he moved to the upper school to be coached for his school certificate. His new form master John Key objected. He told the headmaster Kyffin was so stupid he refused to be responsible for getting him through the school certificate. Happily Kyffin was taken by David Bevan, the best master at the school Bevan was a confident, quiet, kindly person. He taught so well that when Kyffin took his school certificate he got more credits than any other boy in the school. He had dreaded the science and physics papers. Fortunately the examination included a natural science paper in which students were asked to write on the life of the fox the otter and the hare. Countryman Kyffin was in his element but his father was puzzled by his success since his younger son had been getting consistently poor reports. One from Sopwith, the senior English master, was the cruellest: "This boy has no power of lucid thought." "Never have I met a boy with less ability," wrote Banks, the mathematics master. His house master Cuthbert Mitford, a member of the notorious family which produced a series of fascist oddities, was particularly scornful. Kyffin remembers him as an incorrigible idiot who had never grown up and who did nothing but mock and laugh at him. Mitford reported: "He is the despair of all who teach him."

When he saw the results of the school certificate Harry Williams demanded an explanation. The headmaster, a Major Hardy, the father of actor Robert Hardy, replied that he had total confidence in his staff. To this Harry Williams responded, "If you have faith in your staff I have no confidence in the school and I intend to remove him." The result was that Kyffin was moved to a form which consisted of boys who were not going on to do a Higher Certificate.

Amongst them Richard Hillary, who was to become a Spitfire pilot, badly burned and disfigured when his plane crashed. He wrote *The Last Enemy,* one of the finest accounts to emerge from World War II. Kyffin remembered him as a silent, sullen boy. At roll call he stood apart as though he felt himself too good to mix with lesser boys. He was a superb athlete and a very good oarsman, but would not train.

The form was given to a new master, a timid little man called MacEachran who it seemed would be cannon fodder for the young toughs in the form. In the event his passion for poetry was such that it raised a spark in their minds.

Kyffin believes it was certainly MacEachran's inspired teaching which awoke the talent in Hilary that later caused him to write and indeed inspired his own *Across the Straits* and *A Wider Sky.* To MacEachran poems were 'spells' and he later published an

Anthology of Spells. He became a legend at the school.

Another pupil was 'Loopy' Ball. He came from Dublin and was a classmate of Richard Cobb who was to become Professor of Modern French History at Oxford and who researched his subject in France whilst living on the streets. They were outsiders who did odd things. The school chaplain was for ever taking small boys out in his car. Richard Cobb rang him up and said "I am the Bishop of Bulawayo. I have been informed you are behaving in a very wrong way with small boys." "Frightened the life out of him and he behaved better after that," Kyffin recalled.

Cobb and Ball hatched a plan to murder Ball's hated mother by getting her into a baby Austin and pushing her over an Irish cliff near his home in Eire. So far as Cobb was concerned this was just juvenile fantasising. But the term after he had gone to Oxford a fellow undergraduate thrust a paper under his nose which told of the terrible murder of Mrs Ball in Dublin. Loopy had taken an axe to his mother and put her in the back of a baby Austin as he planned. Unfortunately, with Mummy in the back wrapped in a sack, it ran out of petrol in O'Connell Street. A passer-by helped Ball push the car to a petrol station where he filled up and drove for the cliff. Unhappily the approach to the headland was a narrow lane which was blocked with a car with a courting couple inside. Ball had to stay there all night until the couple left and he was able to carry out his plan. He was quickly caught but when he appeared in court a Guarda Inspector called O'Reilly who knew the family spoke in his defence. He said: "It was a very understandable thing for the young gentlemen to do. She was a real old baggage." Ball was given three years and then emigrated to Australia.

For Kyffin the best part of his time at Shrewsbury were visits to his relations, the Ramsays. Betty Mewies was another regular visitor:

> My grandfather's sister Aunt Louisa married Andrew Ramsay, who had been Darwin's geologist on the *Beagle* and Director of the Royal Ordnance Survey. They met when Ramsay was on Anglesey researching for his book, which was the first to date the pre-Cambrian rock strata there.
> They had four daughters, Fanny, Ella, Violet and Dora. All

tremendously eccentric old ladies. But very formal. During the war it didn't matter if you were only having spam for supper you had to dress. As a girl of sixteen I thought it was marvellous to put on a long frock and be complimented by the house keeper and the maids.

Violet always carried a shopping basket with her. It contained her will and her best jewellry. She had two pairs of glasses, one for eating in. She would eat very, very quickly, then take them off and put the other pair on to talk. Dora's little fault was not her glasses but her teeth. Her top set didn't fit. She would very cleverly whip her handkerchief from her pocket and remove the teeth behind its cover. I remember once the teeth fell onto the carpet but everyone pretended they were not there. Dora thought that no-one had ever noticed when she took out her teeth so cleverly and it would have been bad manners to disabuse her.

The other three died but poor old Violet went on living for quite a time. She had a housekeeper called Maggie who was a wicked person who had Violet under her thumb. When Violet died Maggie had inherited their lovely house and its contents.

Artistic tuition was basic at Shrewsbury, though Kyffin retained a great affection for his art master, Woodruffe. In the art room there was a drawer filled with prints. Art lessons consisted of choosing a print and copying it. Kyffin's parents asked Woodruffe to give him private lessons. It paid off. During his last summer term a prize was offered, Hardy's Painting Prize, for work done in the holidays. To Kyffin's astonishment, he won. He was convinced the reason was the headmaster's wife was a relation. He was asked as his prize to choose a book on art. As Ernest Naish reported, above, Kyffin held out for a book on hunting despite the objection of his headmaster.

There were unlooked for consequences of the win. Later in life when he was at loggerheads with Rollo Charles, the Keeper of Art at the National Museum of Wales, Charles told him he had also gone in for the prize that Kyffin had won. Kyffin believed this rivalry was behind the huge differences of opinion he and Charles had over the respective merits of artists.

Despite his prowess, Kyffin had no thought to become an artist. His dream was to join the cavalry. Alas, there was no money left in the family. His grandfather had sold all their land. That meant he also had to abandon his second choice which was to farm. In consolation his father articled him to Yale and Hardcastle a firm of land agents in Pwllheli. At the time he was living with his parents in Abererch. Although he vehemently claims only a desultory interest in art, nevertheless every lunchtime he ran two miles home to paint a quick water colour and then lunchtime over ran a further two miles back to the office.

On Sundays he would leave the house at 2 pm and run to the top of Yr Eifl and run back in time to get to the house for the 6 pm news. It was in this house he began to paint portraits. One was of a neighbour's little daughter, Jane of Ty'n Sarn, Abererch. To put her at her ease Kyffin asked how she had spent the morning.

"Oh we was all go to Pwllheli to buy presents. Tom got a cap. Gwilym got a coat. I got two pairs of knickers."

"What did brother Hughie get?"

"Oh Hughie is going to hospital in Bangor. So Hughie got a Holy Bible."

There was little faith in hospital but much in heaven.

THREE

Captain Jack had been scornful when Kyffin said he was going into a land agents' office. "Sitting about all day with a ledger on your desk and writing down figures." As it happened he joined the firm, Yale and Hardcastle in their office in a passage between High Street and Penlan Street in Pwllheli.

The two partners were an unlikely pairing. George Frederick Cunningham Yale was an aristocrat. Impeccably dressed, he drove round his clients' land as though it were his own. Donald Hardcastle on the other hand was English working class. Kyffin's was not the most arduous of jobs. He was allowed one day off a week for hunting and one day off for shooting over the estates the firm.

Among Kyffin's duties was rudimentary architecture. He designed shippons for tenant farmers all over Lleyn and restored the medieval hall on the 30,000 acre Nant Horon estate. The Nant Horon and Broom Hall estates were the biggest clients of the firm. The Broom Hall estate was founded in the nineteenth century by a farmer, Rowland Jones. It is said that at his funeral there were two carriages, the first contained family mourners, the second contestants of the will.

He had a grandson called Evans who qualified as a solicitor and took a job in London. One day a woman came in seeking a divorce. The firm's principal refused her. Evans who knew the woman, one of William IV's illegitimate daughters, also knew she owned part of Regent Street, Greek Street and part of Golden Square. He offered to win the divorce on condition she marry him. He was a personable young man and the heiress agreed. In consequence, Broom Hall became a very rich estate of 30,000 acres. Their son Colonel Lloyd Evans could walk from Pwllhelli to Caernarfon on his own land

The elder son Rollie was wildly eccentric. He hated the local rector so much he built a platform on the estate wall. Whenever the rector passed, the son climbed on the platform and bellowed at him like a bull. Another son John married an American girl Camille Clifford, one of the famous Gibson Girls.

Kyffin worked for William, the younger son, when he inherited Broom Hall. He was in the navy and served around the world with the Prince of Wales on the *Renown*. Kyffin remembered that William hated the colour red. He was a keen pilot and he would fly over his estate looking for tenants who had used red ridge tiles. If he found one he would land, climb into his Ford V8 drive into Pwllheli and storm into the office ordering the agents to get rid of the tiles. One day taxiing for take off he was blown off course into a bank of soil and killed.

The estate was sold to Billy Butlin, who built a naval air station, HMS Glendower at Pwllheli. After the war he recovered it and opened his first holiday camp there. Butlin tried to ingratiate himself with the locals. He booked the Old Vic theatre company to put on a show in the big house. He invited all the people in Lleyn and sent buses round the villages to pick them up. The excited audience filed into the hall and the performance began. They watched it in total silence. At the end of the evening they all crept away to their buses in a disappointed silence. They had believed they were going to see Vic Oliver, a famous comedian.

At the gateway to the Lleyn stands Glynllifon, a huge estate and the most magnificent neo-classical house in Wales. It was built by the first Lord Newborough who believed his wife was the rightful queen of France. Kyffin loved to tell the story of the last of the family to live in Glynllifon, the Hon Fred Wynn. He had plenty of money, lived as he pleased, and did not give a damn who he offended. He had two nephews. One was Tom (Lord Newborough), a bluff sort of mariner, and the other Colonel Vaughan Wynn, a cavalry officer who had fought in the South African war.

Fred knew they hated each other. He would tell Lord Newborough he was going to inherit. The next week he would tell Vaughan and his wife Ruby the same thing. When he knew he was dying he sent for Vaughan and told him: "You are going to inherit. You might as well get ready. Bring along all your stock to the parkland here." Vaughan danced away with joy and had all his cattle and sheep sent to Glynllifon. Then the dreadful Fred Wynn breathed his last and when his will was proved it read "I leave all my land at Glynllifon and all the stock upon it to my nephew Lord Newborough."

Vaughan had to be content with becoming Tom Newborough's heir. He married three times in a campaign to get a son so that Vaughan would not inherit. One of his wives, Denise, was an Hungarian Jew, madam of a bawdy house in Shepherd's Market, in London. It was all to no avail and the dreaded Vaughan inherited.

During his time Tom Newborough had cost the estate a fortune. He was showing the house to Sir Thomas Merton, a Jewish banker and great lover of the arts. On a dark wall outside the butler's pantry Sir Thomas saw a painting, for which he immediately offered Tom £500. Newborough thought Merton a fool. But he agreed and Merton took away a Botticelli which was subsequently valued at over a million pounds. It is a portrait of a young man holding a medallion which was later used on a poster for a Royal Academy show of Italian treasures.

Kyffin's best friend at the time was Sandy Livingstone-Learmouth, a Hampshire Scot who had married the daughter of a slate mine owner in Blaenau Ffestiniog. Sandy and Kyffin had met after Shrewsbury, and at eighteen Sandy had suggested Kyffin join the 6th Battalion the Royal Welch Fusiliers TA. He did, principally because Sandy said he did he would get some good shooting.

There was no question of working his way through the ranks or facing a selection board. Sandy's word and Kyffin's background were enough to get him commissioned as second lieutenant and appointed second in command of the Pwllheli platoon, which Sandy commanded. In the event, shortly after Kyffin joined, Hitler seized the opportunity to invade Poland and suddenly there were shouting opportunities all over Europe.

It must be said this was not an excessively military formation that Kyffin joined.

> I should not have passed the medical because I had already suffered my first epileptic attack. Luckily the M.O. was drunk. He stood swaying in the doorway, launched himself at me and gave me a terrible punch in the stomach. I went flat on the floor. He stood over me and said
> "Did you feel that?"
> I said "No."
> "Right," he said. "Give me your papers."
> He went into his office, I heard a clink of glass and when he came out he told me I had passed my medical.
> Our men were farm labourers and slaughterhouse attendants. One of them was Willy Christmas Jones. W.C. Jones. There was always a terrible row when the others called him 'Shit-house Jones'. We had another little man we called General Franco because he was the spanish leader's double.
> The augurs of war were not good. We had a sergeant instructor called Nichol of the Welsh Guards. When war broke out he shot himself in the armoury.
> On Sunday 3rd September I had to take Church Parade in Porthmadog. Archdeacon Jenkins spoke from the pulpit: "Doubtless in a few months time you will all be blown to pieces."
> All the soldiers behind me went 'Jesus'.
> When we left Pwllheli to join the company at Porthmadog the word had gone round we were going to India. All the mothers and sisters and wives and girl friends had turned up to wave us off, howling 'We'll never see them again'.
> When we left Porthmadog the mothers and sisters and girl friends came from Pwllheli and Beddgelert and Blaenau Ffestiniog and the word was 'They are going to Egypt. We will never see them again.' We went to Old Colwyn.

The amiable Colonel Davies remembers Kyffin and his friend Sandy coming to Hightown Barracks in Wrexham. The Depot of the Royal Welch had become an infantry training unit. Kyffin got the shooting Sandy Livingstone-Learmont had promised him, though in rather unorthodox fashion. Colonel Davies explained:

> Sandy was a very eccentric person. He introduced a bow and arrow into the Mess. He was very good with it. He always carried a pistol wherever he went. If he saw something in a field he wanted to take a pot shot at he would stop the car, take out his pistol and shoot it.

He and John together made up a series of Crawshay Bailley songs. He has recently published some in a book with his cartoons. But not the ones they sang in the regiment. The other thing I remember about him in those days was his cartoons of brother officers. They were brilliant and the regiment still treasures many of them.

After training in Wrexham Kyffin's Battalion were ordered to Northern Ireland. The Company Sergeant Major, Gwilym Jones, who looked like a Welsh forward, was the landlord of the Red Lion in Porthmadog. When he arrived at the station to embark he was as drunk as a lord. The Adjutant, Major Edward Cadogan, was walking up and down when Gwilym came up the steps dragging his rifle by the spout with the butt banging on the steps. Cadogan started to remonstrate. Gwilym said "Look here. When we get to Ireland I'll bloody get you." Cadogan was speechless with amazement.

Before Cadogan had time to put him on a charge in Northern Ireland, Gwilym went home on compassionate leave. The boat he returned on was torpedoed and he arrived back a hero. He told Kyffin, "There was I in my underpants shaving and a bloody torpedo came right through the ablutions. I came out of the ship riding it like a jockey."

Kyffin, Gwilym and the rest were part of the assembling 53rd Welsh Division. It was to have included a friend of Kyffin's, Philip Stable, the son of a High Court judge, Sir Wintringham Stable. But he had to be moved on quickly when his father sentenced some IRA men to death in Liverpool. Stable senior was another of the characters who seem to have populated Kyffin's Gwynedd. One day he was caught speeding in Bala. After he had made a speech in mitigation the presiding magistrate said "Sir Wintringham, you may remember that last year you came to talk to us about the law. In the course of your talk you told us we must never be bamboozled by legal jargon. Well we are not going to be. We find you guilty." It was Sir Wintringham who, out shooting on a blank day, eventually saw a rabbit cowering in a sheep fold. He raised his gun and was heard to mutter "And not even a Welsh jury is going to get you off this time."

In fact Kyffin's military career was relatively short. His epileptic attacks were becoming more frequent and despite urgent representation to everyone he thought might help, he was invalided out of the army which he loved. Wendy Davies told me: "He always wanted to be a soldier. It was a terrible disappointment when his health broke down and he was invalided out. He was always a weedy looking individual but tough. And he didn't have any fits out hunting."

At the end of his life he was still musing on the cause of the disease. He believed it was the abuse he suffered as a tiny child at the hands of one of the nurses his mother had employed to look after him. Or perhaps it came with the meningitis he contracted when he was fifteen, or when his tonsils were ripped out.

Significant too was this memory from his prep school:

> In the summer there were canoes for hire on the sea below the school. You could either go out on your own or in a pack. One day I went out with Dick and I got into a panic. I was suddenly petrified at the idea of drowning. It had never happened before. It might have had something to do with the epilepsy because epileptics do get unreasoning panics.
>
> I have always had amazing energy. I used to run from the sea at Pwllheli to the top of the Rivals. My doctor says it is due to an in-body supply of LSD. I can paint an eight foot picture in a day which is something no other artist can do. And I feel better at the end of the day. When I get these epileptic attacks – and I still do as sort of shocks – they make me feel awful but they make me paint.
>
> It stimulates the brain and I can paint. I haven't had grand mals for years and years. I get petit mal but if I didn't I wouldn't paint. It's all tied up.
>
> It is odd how epilepsy scares people to death. I would never hide the fact that I was epileptic. Partly because people have felt terribly guilty about being epileptic, especially women, and I wanted to break this. You don't hide the fact that you have arthritis. Even at Highgate School when I was teaching there I heard a couple of masters talking about a boy. One said, "Of course you know he is epileptic and all epileptics are barmy." That attitude does an immense deal of harm. People go through life terrified because they are epileptic. If I talk about it I know other people will feel better for it.

In an odd way Kyffin was grateful for his disease: "I have a feeling it is the clue to all my paintings. I have been compared to

Van Gogh who was also epileptic. It's true we came from the same social background. We both had highly strung mothers, and fathers who were well balanced. We both had brothers who were worshiped by their mothers."

Kyffin's first epileptic fit came in 1937 after shooting on a very cold day, followed by a regimental function at which he had one glass of port,

> I went to bed and the next morning I was found under an open window with snow on me. I must have been struck as I got up to close the window. I had a second attack a few hours later. Sandy drove me home barely conscious. My doctor sent me to Lord Cohen, a very distinguished surgeon with a practice in Rodney Street, in Liverpool. He gave me a lumbar puncture and made a mess of it. He hit the vertebrae and it was unbelievably painful. I was in such pain that when we got to Port Dinorwic I had to be taken out and laid on the floor of the Halfway House.
>
> The next attack came the morning after a dance at the Goat in Beddgelert. On that occasion I had nothing to drink but the next day when I went for my lunch of beans on toast I had an attack in the street.

What is certain is the value of the work which Kyffin did throughout his life to help others suffering from the disease. Miriam Rees worked among epileptics as a social worker. She said, "The epilepsy has meant that Kyffin has missed so much in life because of his illness. But by publicly admitting he suffers from epilepsy he has done a massive amount to help others. Most epileptics hide their disease but Kyffin is never afraid to put his head over the parapet. It takes a lot of doing because the disease frightens other people."

Eileen Evans of Llangoed, Llanrwst ran a support group for epileptics in Bangor. "My son, who was an epileptic, hanged himself when he was thirty. He found he had got nowhere in life. Epilepsy affected his social life, his career, his education, everything. I found him hanging from a banister at his home in Bethesda. My son was intelligent enough to know he was going nowhere in life and he was better out of it. Who knows? Perhaps he was right."

It had a devastating effect on our lives. My husband went

downhill and died. Sufferers desperately want to be treated as normal people. They hate people to hover over them. The problem is that when a carer knows it is possible for them to lose balance in some of the most dangerous situations – in my son's case mountain climbing, even walking by a river – it makes them a nervous wreck. Epilepsy has a devastating effect. I speak from experience. People don't understand it. Someone crashes down, writhing and kicking. It's natural for the people round them to be afraid. People are fine with epileptics until they see them in a fit. From then on they are cagey about being around."

It is not putting it too strongly to say that Mrs Evans worshiped Kyffin from the day she launched the Ysbyty Gwynedd Epilepsy Group and was told he was prepared to be involved. "We immediately struck up a a rapport. I said 'I believe you would be willing to become president'. He said 'Good God no. I don't want to be a figurehead. I will be chairman.'

Typically, Kyffin was hugely active in his new role. Eileen Evans recalls: "It was as much down to the fact that we had such a charismatic chairman as my hard graft that got the association off the ground. He arranged sensational Christmas parties at Plas Mawr in Conwy, Penrhyn Castle and Cochwythan a medieval house, home of Archbishop Williams. Over the fourteen years I ran it I hope we managed to bring the illness out of the darkness and to get people to realise that epileptics are no different from other people."

As part of her work Eileen Evans spent a good deal of time contemplating the position of epilepsy sufferers in society:

> I frankly doubt that epilepsy gives you talent but it is true that Van Gogh, Edward Lear and Julius Caesar were epileptics. I am always loath to attribute anything to such an illness. But the similarities between Kyffin and Van Gogh are there. I have a very large folder containing his letters and cards. On the outside I have written to the children 'Take very great care of the contents. I have no doubt that one day Kyffin will be as famous as Van Gogh'.
>
> To have been recognised to the extent he has in his lifetime is remarkable. I remember that in 1987 on TV an *Antiques Roadshow* expert valued one of his paintings at £14,000. Kyffin has always wondered to me why people buy his paintings. He

doesn't want his paintings to be more than ordinary people can afford.

The higher you go in society the easier it is to hide epilepsy. For the sufferers it is an absolutely dreadful burden. Kyffin started off life free of it. He thinks he had some peculiar episode when he was about seven and then nothing again for years. This often happens. It has affected his career for the best. He is one of the few people who can say illness has given them anything. When he first told me he had got diabetes as well I was devastated because I had been making him birthday cakes. I thought, My God, I could have killed him. There he was with undiagnosed diabetes and I was feeding him great chunks of rich fruit cake. He could have gone into a coma and I would have been responsible for killing-off Wales's most famous artist.

What I find tragic about Kyffin is that he has a great deal of love to give to a person. It was blown up in his face because of his ill health. It got between him and his girl.

He was so understanding and kind and generous to the group. Epileptics are obsessive and it may account for the frenzied rate at which he paints. When they find something they like doing they use it as an escape. It is a sinister illness. Kyffin hunted in the mountains. It takes a lot of bravery. It is easier to live a sheltered life.

I remember him telling me once he had gone to Cwm Bychan to paint and he honestly felt the mountains were coming down on him. To stay there and continue to paint takes tremendous courage.

Lady Crickhowell also suffered from mild epilepsy as a result of an operation which went wrong. She told me: "I take the same drug as Kyffin. Once you find the level of the dosage it is alright and you can live a normal life, even get a driving license as Kyffin and I both have."

Eluned Ann Thomas, a member of the Welsh Language Society, took over the Ysbyty Gwynedd group from Kyffin. When I met her at her home in Bodedern she told me: "Kyffin used his influence to get us a room at the hospital to meet in. His influence is always available when an epileptic needs help. He is a kind and good man. Very gentle. I was surprised that he was so keen on the army. He is so gentle he comes over as a pacifist." Mrs Thomas met Kyffin when she learned of the epilepsy support group in Bangor.

My husband John is an epileptic. We went in and Kyffin was the chairperson. We were unaware of his importance. He is our greatest ambassador because he has never tried to hide his epilepsy. The only time I have seen him angry was when Reginald Bosanquet the TV news reader accidentally disclosed he was an epileptic. Kyffin was furious that he hadn't disclosed it to help combat the fear people have of the disease. There is still prejudice. There is a boy we are trying to help today. He had a fit on the bus from Bangor to his home in Caernarfon. They just threw him off the bus because they thought it was drugs. We get examples of people being barred from shops because they have had *Grand Mals*. My husband John's mother never told anyone he had epilepsy and my father was very upset that I was marrying a sufferer

Imagine what it must have been like when Kyffin was young. It doesn't matter who you are or what you are, he welcomes you to his friendship. We were all heart broken when Eileen's son committed suicide. But I can remember Kyffin saying to me 'I understand his depression'. And I thought 'You probably suffer in the same way'. I think it is the epilepsy that gives Kyffin his energy.

Her contact with him also helped Eluned Thomas draw some conclusions about Kyffin's Welshness: "I do think his mother did him a great deal of harm when she prevented him from speaking Welsh. He is Cymry Cymraeg. Had he been allowed to speak Welsh he would have been another Cynan, our greatest bard. He knows a lot more Welsh than he let's on but I think he is too shy to use it. You can tell his love for the language by the loving way he pronounces the words. He wants people to speak in their mother tongue. Deep down he misses it because he feels so Welsh. As a painter he speaks to people who are not interested in art. The young farmers round here go mad for one of his animal postcards, or a farm print. He understands ordinary people so well."

FOUR

Kyffin returned to civilian life wholly conquered and in his own eyes far from a hero. He had fought a series of impressive battles with medical boards but their verdicts had been unanimous. He had no future as a soldier. It was a crushing blow. Since boyhood Kyffin had wanted to be a professional soldier, ideally in the cavalry. He saw himself leading his men in a do or die charge. Now he realised the nearest he was going to get to war was the Home Guard. He could not even go back to his job as a land agent: the army doctors had told him the examinations would tax him too severely. He did not take seriously their suggestion he could become a painter. That was not a job, It was a hobby.

There was one consolation. When he returned to his home on the Lleyn it was to find that his mother had taken on a Land Girl. A very beautiful Land Girl. Her name was Gwyneth Griffith. The Williamses had no land but Gwyneth, who was between jobs, had agreed to help with the housework while she was looking for a place on a farm. Although he did not realise it at the time it was probably the most important meeting of Kyffin's life. Gwyneth was a brilliant artist and the best student of her year at the Slade School of Art. For the moment, though, it was enough that she was beautiful and moved like a gazelle. Not for the first time Kyffin fell in love.

Unfortunately Mrs Williams noticed and disapproved. Kyffin told me:

> Gwyneth's time with us was fated. There were terrible rows. She was sent packing and went to work at a farm at Llandegai, a big Penrhyn Estate farm at the bottom of the Nantfrancon Pass where she fell deeply in love with a farm boy who seemed to dominate her.

Some years later a doctor in Swansea read *Across the Straits* in which I wrote about her. He wrote to tell me his father had a farm near Bangor and he knew Gwyneth. He came to see me and kept saying what a lovely girl she was. I realised he was the farm boy. He never married her.

Gwyneth was a very sensitive delicately featured girl. Her father came from St Davids and her mother was a Lewis of Montgomeryshire. She was very dreamy and used to wander round in a state of permanent drowsiness. I found her extremely good company but she would have nothing to do with me. She is a lovely gentle girl.

The lovely gentle girl hooted with laughter when Kyffin's words were recounted to her in the ground floor flat near Trefor Bridge in Llangollen, where she lived after retiring from her job as art mistress at a girl's school in the town,

He wouldn't think that if he could see me now at 83. I was very cross with him when he wrote in *Across the Straits* about me moving like a gazelle. I was teaching at the time and they gave me a terrible time in the common room.

It is true I had been at the Slade and I got on well there. But I was too lazy to be an artist. I won a prize but I have never had any respect for my work. I never hang my own paintings in the flat. To be honest the idea of being shut up in a studio repelled me. My grandmother was a farmer's wife and I wanted to farm. As a young girl I said if I couldn't farm I wanted a job with animals. Painting came a very bad third, something John could never understand. We did lots of things together but I never realised he was sweet on me. In fact I don't think he really understood women

I know he was very disappointed that I was not as interested in painting as he was. I had pretty well given it up. I took my paints and easel round the farms I worked at. But I did not even unpack them.

I remember once he took me sketching to Nantperis. He had his sketch book and a bottle of ink and was soon drawing away. I didn't even take mine out. I just stood there shivering, wishing he would take me for a cup of tea. I was certainly not a compulsive painter in the way that he is. But I always enjoyed his company. He was great fun.

He loved shooting rabbits and insisted on teaching me. We began with clay pigeons and when he thought I was ready he took me out with a gun looking for a sitting target. We found one at last but I was very reluctant and by the time I had brought the gun up I was glad to see the sitting target had run off. He was not pleased.

Yet it was Gwyneth who launched him on his career:

> I saw some water colours he had painted. I was very impressed and I advised him to contact the Slade. In fact I wrote to the Head of the School, Professor Randolph Schwabe, recommending him. Mrs Williams was a very possessive woman and it was a long time before she forgave me for getting him into the Slade and taking him away from home.
>
> I believe she did him a great deal of harm. I remember once we were sitting by the Menai Strait and he said 'I can never marry. I am epileptic.' I had never heard that epilepsy was a bar to marriage but his mother had told him he must never marry. His father wouldn't have said anything. I am afraid he just did as he was told.
>
> When he was at the Slade, John wrote to say he was worried about his mother living alone after her husband died. He asked me to move in with her but I refused. It would not have done.

She looked wistful when she said "All I have to remind me of him is a sketch he gave me. I went to his studio determined to buy one. On the wall was this lovely rockscape with waves crashing against them and over all a setting sun. I asked how much it was and he said £500 which was beyond my pocket. I looked through some sketches and came across one that was obviously a preliminary sketch for the rockscape. He gave it to me and it has been on my wall ever since. I know he thought the Arts Council was against him but when I was teaching I met an Arts Council official who thought he was a fine man and a great painter. But he said rather wistfully 'I do wish he wouldn't teach people to paint like he does.' I knew what he meant. Kyffin looks easy to imitate but his imitators cannot put that extra piece of magic into the picture that Kyffin can."

Kyffin was astonished at the idea of going to art school. He had no wish to be an artist. If he could not be a soldier or a land agent he would settle for a job as a school master. He went to Gabbitas and Thring to try to get a job in a prep school and whilst awaiting an appointment took a job with Windsor and Newton as a salesman. No job materialised.

When he was offered an interview for the Slade he was astonished. The letter asked for examples of his work. He had none but his sketchbooks, so he copied a Paul Nash painting of widgeon winging over marshes from a cigarette card and sent that. He was amazed to receive a letter giving him an interview with the school which at that time had been evacuated to Oxford. Afterwards he always explained his success by saying it was wartime and the Slade had very few male students.

Kyffin recalled "I stayed in a pub in Oxford and went for my interview the next day. Schwabe was a very well mannered man but he looked horrified when I showed him my sketch books. However, he offered me a place and in a sort of dream I accepted it."

At Oxford the Slade was merged with Ruskin School of Art and had two professors, Schwabe and Albert Rutherstone who had been Master of Drawing at Ruskin. It was housed in a wing of the Ashmolean and the ratio of girls to men was eight to one.

Kyffin joined the school in October 1941. He lodged in Observatory Street with the Singletons, a glorious if feckless Irish family with a son who played the saxophone incessantly. Kyffin was told he was a little odd in consequence of a Dublin coalman emptying a sack of coals on his head

From the first day Kyffin believed Schwabe had made a mistake.

> It was terrifying because all these girl students could draw like angels and lots of them looked like angels too. I had never really drawn at all and I just could not do it. We had a thing called the Sketch Club. Students were encouraged to do their own work and send it in to be judged.
>
> The tutor in charge of the Sketch Club was a man called Barnet Freedman. He was a bully. He was terribly rude to the girls. He would go up to their easel and say "I suppose the colour is alright and the drawing and the composition. Do you know what I think you ought to do with it?" Then he would pause and add 'Put it under the sink and stand on it.'
>
> With me he was even ruder. I went up to Boar's Hill outside Oxford and did three water colours. I put them on the dais with the work of the other students. When Freedman came along to criticise he said "When I first saw these I said Great Scott. When

I looked for a second time I said Good Lord. When I saw them a third time I said Heaven Help him." I stayed away for a week after that.

Fortunately Alan Gwyn Jones also taught at the Slade. He was a wonderful artist and I learned a lot from him. He was a descendant of John Jones, the regicide, and won the DSO with the Welsh Guards. One of the finest portrait painters in Britain, he could never get a exhibition in Wales. The Arts Council said they had never heard of him. Then at the end of his life, just as he was going blind, the Tate gave him a retrospective. That woke the Arts Council. They gave him one too. At the Swansea Eisteddfod he won the gold medal and a week later he died.

Kyffin insisted drawing did not come easily. "I had to learn. All the others were good before they went there. They went there because they had talent. I went there for the good of my health. I couldn't draw. I did win a couple of portrait prizes but I can't think how. I got the Robert Ross Leaving Scholarship of £10. Sheer nepotism. I got on very well with Professor Schwabe because I shared my lodgings in Observatory Street with his sister-in-law. One day I was walking along the High with him and he stopped and said 'Oh Williams. I have got a scholarship. I always forget to give it. Would you like it?' I said 'Thank you very much'."

Tom Griffiths, who was at Slade with Kyffin, recalled at his London flat that Kyffin was a loner:

> Coming from the army he was older than most of us at Slade. He did not join a group, let alone a gang, so we weren't really aware of him. He has said he drifted through Slade. Of course, he did much more. Like all artists he took what nourishment he needed. He took as much of Slade drawing as he needed and did not become a slave to pretty line as most of us did.
>
> William Coles, whom John wrote about as Maurice Wood in *A Wider Sky,* was a bit older than the average and became a good friend of his. He once made a perceptive and appreciative remark to me about John's work. He thought he had much natural facility and where others might have come to rely on superficial effects he deliberately made challenges for himself, one of which was using the palette knife which was a most un-Slade approach.
>
> William Cole had a deep feeling for tonal values, another un-Slade virtue, and I think John was usefully influenced by this while always remaining true to himself. If he appeared to drift it

was because most of his fellow students could not have appreciated his stickability – more important in the long run than
fashionable cleverness. Actually he was by no means a tortoise. As
the rapidity of his cartoons and his decisive mastery of character
in portraiture show. He was much cleverer both as an artist and
a man than we other students appreciated in our self absorption.
Both Randolph Schwabe and Albert Rutherstone liked him and
became good friends. They were not fools.

Kyffin thought he knew why he was improving, "I was lucky
because unlike the rest of the students at the Slade I knew exactly
what I wanted to paint. The land where my family had lived for a
thousand years. Other people who were far better artists were
floundering around trying to get the effects of light which was
quite beside the point. I never worried because I knew I hadn't
any talent. When everything was very frustrating to begin with I
wasn't all that bothered by early failure."

To Kyffin the student, art was a skill, reproducing on paper
something you see before you. All that changed one day in the
Ashmolean Library when he took down a book on Piero della
Francesca.

> I turned over the pages mechanically until I came to a sudden
> stop. There was Piero's 'Resurrection' with the sublime figure of
> Christ rising from the tomb above the sleeping soldiers. My
> initial reaction was shock followed by a feeling of intense
> emotion. I gazed at this beautiful picture until I could no longer
> see it for my tears which were rolling down my cheeks
>   It was the amazing compassion which Piero had managed to
> put into the eyes of Christ. Here was a face of such strength and
> love that for the first time I began to realise what great art is. An
> intangible thing, impossible to rationalise, and far removed from
> mere representation.

In that moment Kyffin the artist was born. "It totally changed my
artistic life. I realised there was something more to painting. There
was a spiritual element which is indefinable. It was a power to
move. It wasn't the religious aspect. It was the beauty of the painting. Because of that I stumbled on. I was heartened when I
learned that St Paul was an epileptic too. His conversion on the
road to Damascus has all the aspects of an epileptic fit with lights
and visions."

Rosalie Williams, the daughter of wealthy parents arrived at the Slade a year after Kyffin. At her home in Lewes, Sussex, she recalled that, after a strict upbringing by a governess, the Slade was a cultural shock.

> I disapproved of girls going into men's rooms and a lot the behaviour was very strange to me. There was also a certain amount of hostility because I came from a wealthy background. I didn't flaunt it. My best friend Yvonne Hudson came from a poor background. We lived together on the college barge and did fire-watching duties for 1s 6d an hour. Kyffin once told me he remembered a dress I wore at the Slade Ball. I am not surprised. I wore the same dress every year.
>
> He wasn't like the other students. He was never arrogant and didn't look down on us because we were girls. We didn't have what is nowadays called a relationship but we were very close. I am very slow to make friends and he kept his emotions to himself. But I liked his attitude as a student. He was serious and he worked hard. It was obvious that he had a great talent. He had to work at his drawing I know but some people have facile talent. They explode like a firework and you think they are going to do great things. But they just disappear. Kyffin developed slowly and greatly. I go to all his exhibitions.

After she left the Slade Rosalie married a well known actor in his day, Hugh Sinclair. "We saw a lot of Kyffin and Hugh liked him as much as I did." Alas, Hugh died suddenly. Rosalie remembers Kyffin was a tower of strength:

> He was always there when I needed him.
>
> I was very surprised when he proposed we should marry. Fond though I was of him it would have been impossible.
>
> I had a very close and happy marriage and Hugh had died suddenly. I had to accustom my children to the loss of their father. I felt I couldn't uproot them from everything they knew with its associations with their father and take them to live in Wales. Of course it would have been quite unthinkable to take Kyffin out of Wales.

Her son Nicholas, an art photographer to whom Kyffin was godfather, says that he would have made a wonderful father: "He was always there for me as he was for my mother. He helped me in my career and all his life was a wonderful friend. He was incredibly warm when my father died. He used to phone and visit regularly. He painted my portrait when I was nine years old. My mother always said he was the nicest person of all the students when she was at the Slade."

To a deeply susceptible man like Kyffin, the Slade where men were in a minority was a honey trap:

> I was unofficially engaged to a lovely girl called Leila Troup but after a year at the Slade she went off to join the WRNS
>
> She took me to her home in Hampshire. It was disastrous. Her father was a very nice man, Chairman of the Hampshire War Agricultural Committee. Her mother was Russian and the least intelligent member of the Moscow intelligentsia. She was a snob. She had been told all Welshmen were common. Her husband who had been wounded in Gallipoli had developed epilepsy and she was determined her daughter would not marry a Welsh epileptic. She forced her to marry someone else. I don't think I ever got over it.
>
> The engagement was never formalised because her parents would never allow it. but what followed has always baffled me because as students we got on well and we were deeply in love. Yet she has never since, in all her life, had one word of praise for anything I have ever done. I do not know why this is. It wasn't that she didn't like me. She will never let go of me. But still after all these years she never ever says anything favourable to me. She comes to all my exhibitions and just laughs at my paintings. It is some strange inhibition. It still hurts because one likes in one's life to have something said if you have something done.

In 1998 Leila, at her home in Blockley, Gloucestershire, was puzzled by his words. She insisted she had always known of his promise and dedication. She told me "It has been marvellous to watch his success and to see his health improve. We saw him for the last time last year when he called in on his way to Highgrove. Prince Charles had invited him to see his pictures. We wiped his car and generally tidied him up. He seemed to enjoy it very much."

She recalled how they had met in the Ashmolean and spent romantic hours together firewatching on the top of the building. "I adored him but the war interfered with long term plans and my mother. She disliked the idea of her future son-in-law being a poor art student. I was never taken to meet his parents but he used to come to my Hampshire home for week ends and I recall we spent a lot of time walking. I think in his London days he missed the sea and the open places. He did one curious picture at this time which consisted of three heavy lines of paint. Blue (sky) red (poppies) and green (fields) which did not impress us very much."

Whilst at eighty he cheerfully admitted that he was still susceptible to a pretty face, Kyffin insisted he was not attractive to women, in considerable opposition to the evidence it should be added. Nevertheless he claimed "It's been a total mystery to me. I always thought I would be a good husband and father. The trouble is I can never show off. I did not court very well. Some men pretend they are nicer than they really are to impress the opposite sex. I felt they should accept me for what I was and they never did."

The real reason that Kyffin did not marry was much darker. His epilepsy held him back. "That has been my tragedy," he told me. Lord Crickhowell, the son of Ralph Edwards who gave Kyffin one of his early breaks and about whom more later, recognised the problem:

> But I think because of his epilepsy Kyffin decided that marriage was not for him. Later there were people who would have married him but by then he had taken, I think a conscious decision.
>
> A deeply susceptible man, Kyffin would rather have been a husband and father than a painter. At best painting offered a way of escape from his epilepsy. In real life there was no escape.

Kyffin himself admitted:

> My priority in life was always to get married. Painting was not then a priority. I have always loved women. It is strange that the two girls I very badly wanted to get married to both had fathers who were epileptic. There was Leila and a German girl. The extraordinary thing about her was that I knew from the moment I met her that she was illegitimate. How I do not know. Her father and mother lived in Geneva and he had been in the German army. She used to come over from Switzerland to see me. On one visit she told me she had just learned that her mother was not her real mother. Apparently during the war in an air raid on Berlin a

girl appeared at her family home with a bundle which she gave to her father. She said 'This is your daughter', and disappeared. When I knew her she was still racked with guilt about the German treatment of the Jews. While she was studying in the medical school in Geneva she met an American Jewish doctor and she married him.

Kyffin believed that in terms of romance his life had been one of near misses:

I have had lots of girl friends but when it came to the crunch they all ran.

When I was at the Slade Jack Baer, who owned the Hazlitt Gallery, would come in to draw. He is now the most respected art dealer in London. His cousin Derek married Roger Williams Evans's cousin Elizabeth. I was terribly in love with her too but I was having epileptic attacks in quick succession.

The truth is girls despised me in those days. They told me I hadn't any health, I hadn't any money and I hadn't any talent. They were right on all three points. In those days I really had no talent at all. Talent comes out through obsession. You can never create obsession. But if you have obsession you can create talent. I had obsession. It was to put down the mountains on canvas or paper. It still is. The people, the landscape and the sea. It started out hunting and having a sort of mental computer that stores images you can recall later. It's a very odd thing. You can train yourself to have a visual memory. It's like having a TV screen in your head that you can turn on at will. But that only comes with experience and continual thinking.

Another odd thing is that I could create my own music in my head and hear the individual instruments playing. Very often I could do this on the underground or on horseback. Movement would turn it on and I could listen for hours to my own music. I couldn't write it down because I do not know a note of music. I played the piano very badly but it was very gratifying to be able to listen to my own music.

Unlucky in love Kyffin was equally unlucky in war. He was desperate to test his courage in action and just once it seemed he had a chance.

A very nice Australian Air Force man called Bill Morrison came to draw in the Slade. He knew I felt guilty about being invalided out when my generation was fighting. One day he said 'We are going out on exercise in the North of Scotland. We are going to bomb an island, would you like to come?' I said 'It sounds rather fun'. He said 'Put on your uniform and come along to the airfield. I will get you in a Wellington. No-one will know.'

He got a crew to keep the officers occupied while he smuggled me into the bomb bay. The engine started turning. I waited for the take off. Suddenly I heard a bellowing below and I was hauled out.

The next week he went on a raid and never came back.

We students used to go to an aircraft dump on the Iffley road, to examine the wrecks of Dorniers, Messerschmitts, Heinkels.

I remember seeing Paul Nash out there, wrapped up in mufflers because he was terrified of catching cold. He was drawing them for his finest paintings, those of planes washed up on the shores of England.

Desperate to play some part in the war his generation were fighting, Kyffin joined the North Company of Oxford Home Guard. The platoon he commanded was as eccentric a body of men as any army ever held since Falstaff's company of hirelings.

One of his soldiers, Haford Gregory who would never come to Sunday parades. Kyffin rooted him out in Jesus College and ordered him to parade the next Sunday. Gregory demurred: "It is more than my life is worth. My father runs the Lord's Day Observance Society in Wales." Kyffin who knew the army planned to test the Home Guard by mounting an invasion on Oxford the next Sunday insisted. He said: "Gregory was the most bloodthirsty soldier of all. I saw him climb on the roof of a tank hammering on the top with the butt of his rifle. Odd how the theological students were usually the fiercest soldiers."

Kyffin's platoon sergeant, Charles Parker, was a dandy who wore a beautifully cut barathea uniform instead of the harsh serge army issue. He loved lecturing on the bren gun and dismantled the gun with tender care. But he refused when Kyffin, by then President of the Slade Society, asked him to lecture the students on old master drawings, on which he was greatest living authority. He replied that he never gave lectures. He was the man, incidentally, who discovered the Tom Keating forgeries

Corporal Atkinson, who was in charge of the armoury, had been a captain in the South African war and a sergeant in the First World War. He was a distinguished military historian of Exeter

College, and a very eccentric man, subject to violent hatreds. One was women students. He would not tolerate them. When they came to his lectures he would address them as gentlemen. He sometimes took his trousers down in their presence and warmed his bottom at the fire. Another hatred was of Brasenose men. He had a series of black cocker spaniels called Jumbo. He would take them onto the wall of Brasenose and set them on the students. The dogs came to know all the Brasenose men and used to bite them in the street.

Kyffin recalled that "My Uncle Jack Kyffin, who lived in Oxford, was a fellow member of the Home Guard. He had been a colonel in the RAMC in World War One and a great boxer who won his last fight at sixty. Although he always claimed he won because his opponent was a corporal who could not bear to strike an officer, a court martial offence in other circumstances. In the Home Guard, although he was merely a medical orderly with the rank of private, it did not deter him from putting his commanding officer on a charge for being late."

Kyffin's platoon was nothing if not enthusiastic. He recalled with a shudder the night they went too far. "We were doing exercises at night and we came across a caravan that a pair of loves were using. One of my platoon threw a thunderflash under the caravan and out dashed a man in his underpants and a woman in her nightie."

With such distractions it was a wonder that Kyffin was able to make the progress he did with his art. Somehow he managed to scrape through his first terms and was told he could stay for another year.

He was barely back in Oxford before deeper more personal disruptions engulfed him. His father died after an attack of bronchitis, and not for the first time his mother's behaviour baffled him. He wrote in *Across the Straits*, "After the burial service she entertained the mourners as if she were presiding over a normal tea party. I felt sure that as soon as it was over she would crack, but she didn't. From that day on she never mentioned his name again and she seemed to want to forget him as she went back into the world of her father."

Back at the Slade, Kyffin received a letter from the commanding officer of a battle school in the south of England. Two days earlier his beloved brother Dick had stepped on a bakelite percussion hand grenade and blown off his left foot. With a shock Kyffin recalled that on the same day his own left foot had unaccountably swollen and he had been in agony for twelve hours until it had just as suddenly subsided. Later his brother told him this apparently telepathic communication had happened half an hour before his own accident.

Kyffin claimed that there was little tuition at the Slade in his day. He recalled Professor Borenius, a shy, gentle man and desperately uncommunicative. His voice in lectures on the History of Art was so soothing that many of his students fell asleep. And his examinations were a farce Kyffin claimed. He would arrive in the lecture hall, immaculate in morning coat, with twelve lantern slides which he would flash onto a screen in turn The students were required to date the painting on the screen, ascribe them to a school and identify the painter. They formed groups and each student took a different period on which he boned up. As a painting flashed on the screen so the student identified it for his friends. Everyone took first class honours in History of Art.

In the life classes there was always a shortage of models and it fell to Kyffin to tour Oxford, press ganging and bribing to provide them. But there were consolations. On one memorable day Lord Berners came in to draw next to him. He went to a lecture by Jan Masaryk and met refugees like Leonid Pasternak, Boris's father and a very good painter indeed. He made a friend of the cartoonist H.M. Bateman, who sat at the next pig to Kyffin drawing deeply serious life studies. He told Kyffin that the war had killed his sense of fun and he could not draw the caricatures for which he was internationally famous. Nevertheless he drew a memorable one of Kyffin in which he looks like a dodgy car salesman or racing tout. Kyffin loved it.

Kyffin believed his own drawing was going on slowly. One day Professor Schwabe had looked at one, sighed heavily and said "Oh Williams, why do you always make your nudes look like oak trees? You cannot draw, you had better see if you can paint."

It was the beginning of the greatest love affair in Kyffin's life.

He wrote years afterwards "I found the rich pigment appealed to my sensuous nature. As I tackled my first life painting I fell completely under the spell of paint and produced something which, even if it was incompetent, was unlike anything else in the school. The more I painted the more I realised that this was my real means of expression. When my third year came to an end I won the Slade Portrait Prize."

FIVE

Kyffin left the Slade with two ambitions: to become and art teacher in a public school and to marry a delightful wife. As was to happen so often in his life, the hour produced the man. Though, alas, not the woman.

His Home Guard Commander, Major Greswell was the secretary of the Oxford University Appointments Board. On Kyffin's behalf he wrote glowing letters to every public school in the country. A considerable number expressed interest and Kyffin began a scholastic tour in order to sell himself.

Sadly, selling himself was never one of Kyffin's talents. Aiming high the first school he tried was Harrow because the head master, R.H. Moore, had been an assistant master at Shrewsbury in Kyffin's day. In his office there was what Kyffin took to be a mat in front of the fire. Only when the mat got to its feet, staggered across the room and bit him did he realise it was an elderly cocker spaniel. Obviously sharing the dog's opinion, Moore turned his old pupil down.

Hearing that the assistant art master of Christ's Hospital was about to be sacked he tried there. He was turned down. At his next attempt, Merchant Taylors, he was shortlisted but in the end the job went to his rival who, it turned out, was the former assistant art master at Christ's Hospital.

He was successful at last when he went for an interview at Highgate School. Geoffrey Bell, the headmaster, was a genial man and took to Kyffin at once. He not only got the job. He was appointed to command the signals platoon of the school Officers' Training Corps. It proved to be a sinecure. All the boys were knowledgeable about radio. Kyffin was not. So he let the platoon run itself, which it did with considerable efficiency.

Delighted with his luck in at last getting a job as an art master, Kyffin went to the Royal Academy to look at paintings. There he met his Slade tutor, Barnet Freedman, to whom he broke the news. Freedman, characteristically discouraging, said "Well, that is you finished as an artist." "I have to teach. I have no money," Kyffin explained. "No artist worth his salt ever worried about money," was Freedman's bald response. Telling the story of this cruel snub many years later the generous Kyffin had to add "that for all his faults Freedman was a fine artist who did some marvellous illustrations for Siegfried Sassoon's *Memoirs of an Infantry Officer.*"

Kyffin's salary for teaching six days a week was £300 a year. It would have gone up to £350 if he had taken a House. "Couldn't do it," he admitted. "It was bad enough spending days with boys. To spend the nights as well would have been hell. I couldn't even bear to eat with them. I used to go into Highgate village to a little café."

The boys had a good opinion of Kyffin, who did not believe that art and punishment were compatible and so refused to punish. But the more anarchic of his pupils began to play on this belief. One day when he told the class how the National Gallery's art collection had been moved to Wales for safety it erupted with laughter. With difficulty Kyffin won silence and asked what was so funny. "Oh sir," said one boy. "It wouldn't be very safe there." "Why not?" enquired Kyffin. "Well sir, you know the rhyme. Taffy was a Welshman, Taffy was a thief."

The torment only lasted a year. By then even the small boys he taught realised that Kyffin was something special and his lessons were among the most popular in the school. That remained true during the twenty-seven years he taught there.

One boy asked if he was married and was told he wasn't. "I thought not," he said. ""You are always so cheerful." Another said "Oh Mr Williams, I understand you are the greatest living artist." "Stuff and nonsense," said Kyffin. "Who on earth told you that?" "Sir, the postman in Taplow."

When a boy behaved really badly he would ask his house master to flog him.

A boy called Winterbottom just would not stop talking. I asked his housemaster John Coombes to flog him. He said I cannot beat Winterbottom. His father is going to get me two tickets for the Cup Final.

I taught Warren Mitchell's son. A nice lad. Swings and round-abouts. Had another boy, Pickering, who was incorrigibly naughty. One night he shinned out down a rope. Part of Hampstead Lane was up and there were lights surrounding the hole. Pickering moved the lights and a car went into the hole. The Head arranged to have him moved to another school. I saw him later. He said "Oh sir, it's not a patch on Highgate. The discipline is appaling."

When I was leaving a little boy came up and said "You cannot leave. you are the best master in the whole school. You never punish anybody."

A boy would ask "Please sir, how do horses go sir?" I would say "Take a pair of spectacles and a couple of round things." "How do cows go?" "Do a rectangle." If a boy asked what he should draw I would think of an animal I knew how to draw and pressurise, say, an elephant into a boy's mind.

Some of his pupils had dazzling careers: "Hoffnung left the term before I came, but Geoffrey Palmer, the actor, was a pupil. I did the scenery for a school production of *Journey's End*. Palmer was in it with Christopher Moran, who directed *Jewel in the Crown* for TV. Two other pupils, Anthony Green and Patrick Proctor, are both Royal Academicians.

I didn't teach Proctor anything. When he came to leave he took me out to tea to tell me what an awful art master I was. A few years later he brought his portfolio and said he was anxious to become an artist. He went to the Slade and within three years he had his first one man show. His pictures filled every gallery in the Redfern and everything was sold before the exhibition opened. I did produce some good boys in my time but I thought the reason was less to do with me than that Highgate drew on a highly intel-ligent area. Bright boys.

Two more of my pupils, John Taverner and Howard Shelley, are now well known musicians. At Highgate all available money went on music, very little on art. The modern side was run by a left winger called Thomas Fox. He would get off the bus every morning and walk in through the school gates reading a book and shaving. Robert Atkins, who never seemed to me very bright, became a cabinet minister.

John Coombes, the housemaster to whom Kyffin turned to administer corporal punishment, recalled: "Kyffin was a wonderful teacher to any boy who had talent. If they had no talent he did not bother with them. One of the more talented boys painted a mural of a fishing village which covered the art room attic walls and ceilings. It was very good."

Kyffin always recalled his pupils with pleasure. "Anthony Howard was a pupil of mine in the junior school. His closest friend was a boy called Cohen. They used to argue endlessly and I remember Howard's short trousers were a damn sight longer than anyone else's. His father was Vicar of Highgate."

Tony Howard, a CBE now, a distinguished biographer and one of the country's leading political journalists, remembers Kyffin with warmth:

> I must have been his worst pupil, never having had the slightest talent for drawing or painting. With his moustachios and ample fair facial hair he struck us all as a very exotic character bringing a breath of fresh air into the rather stale and sterile wartime air of that institution.
>
> I remember him coming to tea in the Vicarage at Highgate on VE DAY in 1945. There had been a Victory service in the forecourt of Highgate School and I suppose my father, a very hospitable man, must have seen him there and asked him to come along. I remember I was slightly taken aback. He had not as a later master at Westminster did, banished me from his art class but I was only too aware of my maladroit efforts in the subjects which he taught. He was, however, charm itself, and no reference at all was made to my being a far from satisfactory pupil.
>
> I think the general view in the school was that he was a slightly eccentric figure, but this was at the start of a very long career at Highgate and I have no doubt that by the end of it he had become an icon. By the end of the war most of the masters were in their dotage and as a youthful member of the staff he was pretty exceptional.

Kyffin would go to enormous lengths to provide facilities for his boys. Coombes said "He felt that if we were to be a proper public school we should have a base for sketching in Snowdonia and adventure holidays. His friend, Sandy Learmont, owned a house and outbuildings in Cwm Pennant, and Kyffin persuaded the Head to buy it for £500." The school still uses the house. In retirement in Betws Garmon, Coombes runs it.

Reminded of his efforts, Kyffin recalled an embarrassing time when he was in Bangor on a dull day and the sun suddenly broke through. He thought he would paint in the Glyders and climbed Devil's Kitchen in his ordinary clothes without any equipment thus breaking all the rules of mountaineering. He was sitting under a rock drawing happily when he saw a Highgate School party, correctly dressed for the mountains coming towards him.

Coombes remembers a sadder occasion. "Kyffin had scripted a school concert to raise funds for a new arts building. He was dressed as a Crimean soldier singing 'Goodbye Dolly Gray' when my mother sitting in the front row collapsed. Kyffin jumped from the stage, bundled her into his Volkswagen and took her to hospital, then came back and finished his song as though nothing had happened."

More happily he remembers a tennis match in which he partnered Kyffin. "When we lost the first set six-one Kyffin said 'There is only one thing to do. We must attack and smash them.' He certainly smashed them. He hit the next ball out of the court, the school and probably Highgate beyond. We lost that set six-love."

War brought some bizarre masters to the school. Predictably Kyffin got on well with them, especially the most exotic of all his colleagues. The P.T. master Prince Fethi Sami was a member of the Ottoman Dynasty which had ruled Turkey for five hundred years. His family were forced out of Turkey when, with the blessing of Lloyd George, the Greeks landed at Smyrna. The Samis who were known to be pro-British were turned out of their palaces by a Turkish mob and forced to flee to the South of France where Sami became an Olympic standard boxer. The family did not give up their Balta Liman Palace on the shores of the Sea of Marmara lightly. As a boy of thirteen, Sami had been given a rifle and told by his father Prince Sami Nedjib to stay at his post until he died. In the event, a British cruiser arrived and took off the family but they had only two hours to pack and could take little with them.

The family loved all things British because they believed the

British were the fairest race on the planet. Sami remembered a British submarine surfacing in the Sea of Marmara next to a boat selling water melons. At pistol point the skipper demanded the whole cargo, which he paid for in gold. Germans were less well liked as Kyffin recalled:

> Sami's father, a captain in the Turkish Lancers, was escorting a German officer who was inspecting his troop. The German slapped a soldier whose button was undone. The Prince said "I do not advise you to do that to a Turkish soldier." The German said a German office was frightened of nothing and when he saw a second soldier with his belt undone he punched him in the stomach. But a third soldier he slapped picked up his rifle and shot the German dead.
>
> When they came to the South of France they were penniless and lived over a garage. The Royal Family had owned two oil wells which they rented to an entrepreneur Nicolai Gulbenkian. When they were deposed he stole them and became one of the richest men in the world. Gulbenkian wore a rare orchid in his buttonhole which was replaced every day. He had his own specially rebuilt London taxi which he famously said would turn on a sixpence "Whatever that is".
>
> Sami loved Anglesey. He said the Menai Strait reminded him of the Bosphorous.

There were plenty of other notable figures on the staff at Highgate School. Kyffin recalls:

> Another teacher, Paddy Ardisher, was a jade merchant in peace-time. John Llywelyn Thomas was a wrangler and a very fine mathematician. His father John Thomas was Queen Victoria's harpist.
>
> Young John was at Harrow with Samuel Hoare who became a cabinet minister. When Hoare came to Highgate to open the new science building John, who didn't realise the loudspeaker was switched on, said "There's old Sam. As big a bloody fool as ever." It echoed over the school.
>
> The school evacuated to Westward Ho, but returned just before the V1 raids began. We had a master, Edward Bullen. Totally rotund and inevitably known as The Egg. Wherever he went to live he was followed by a flying bomb. He was bombed out of two new houses in Highgate and finally bombed whilst conducting a lesson. He was discovered underneath a blackboard wondering how Hitler always knew where he was. He asked me

to dinner with another man called Charlie Benson. Sure enough, in the middle of the dinner, the sirens went, we heard a flying bomb. Happily it failed to find him and the jinx was broken.

Despite such colourful colleagues, life at a school is scarcely the milieu for an artist and even leafy Highgate a poor exchange for the North Wales mountains in which he had rejoiced. How did Kyffin stick it?

> No option. I wasn't selling pictures. I would rather have taught in an art school but no art school would have me.
> I wanted to teach in an art school because there were girls. I tried every art school in Britain but none would have me because by then I could draw.

Nevertheless, after two years teaching the whole week, the need for time to paint became unbearable. When he explained he would have to leave, the headmaster Bell asked, "Do you have a father who can give you a private income?" Kyffin admitted he had not. "Then you are an idiot to think of giving up an income. Why not get a friend to share the job?" Kyffin brought in a Slade friend and a brilliant painter, William Coles. He taught for three days and painted for four. It was hard living:

> My sole income was £200. I had not only to live on that I had to buy paint. My salary went up but when I left twenty-seven years later in 1973 I was only getting £1,900 a year as senior arts master.
> By that time I was selling a few pictures. But the early years were rough. I used to gamble in a secondhand bookshop in Highgate village. Twice a week in the evenings after the shop closed all the runners – the men who bought books to sell them on again – assembled and the two rogues, Fisher and Spurr, who ran it, had gambling sessions. I used to play table tennis there and stay to gamble.
> I wouldn't play poker but I knew if I stuck to Rummy I would win two shillings. That was enough to have an omelette and chips at a café on Highgate Hill.
> I couldn't eat in my lodgings. My landlady was blind and couldn't really manage the cooking. She would give me breakfast but I remember once the kippers were cooked in the newspaper they had been wrapped in at the shop.

He was poor in the way few people are now. Many of his works were snowscapes. Not from choice; Flake White is the cheapest oil paint. But he insisted "The extraordinary thing is that I never worried about not having enough money, although I am a terrible worrier and, like my mother, perpetually filled with apprehension."

> The school was endlessly good to me. When I left in 1973 I was succeeded by a man whom Bell's successor as headmaster, Alfred Boulton, allowed me to choose myself. Peter Greenham Keeper of the Royal Academy had been at school with Boulton. I asked Peter for someone for Highgate and he produced Gordon Tweedale. When I met Tweedale at the school gate he was wearing a magenta suit with an emerald green lining. I thought 'Oh My God what will Fred say?'
>
> In the event Alfred took a liking to him and he was an absolutely howling success. Far better than me. He wasn't mixed up with a desire to be a painter. He had time for all the little perishers and what is more he had a wife who did pottery. A boy came to see me years later. He told me that Gordon Tweedale had the most successful department in the school.

Kyffin was very fortunate in the picture framer he found; Robert Siole was one of the finest framers in Europe. Yet Siole was not his real name. He was C.L. Roberts but took the name Siole because it sounded French and was good for trade. He was in fact Liverpool Welsh and a man of many parts. He had been a pilot in the Royal Flying Corps in World War One. He was shot down over enemy lines and taken prisoner. Whilst in the camp he and some fellow prisoners worked up an act as chorus girls. They became so good at it that when they came home they auditioned for the Windmill Theatre. After some time he met and married Annette Mills, who was to go on to international fame as the creator of the TV puppet Muffin the Mule. With Annette he worked up a speciality dancing act and, according to the poet John Ormond, it was they who introduced the Charleston to Britain. Roberts had seen it in South America when he toured there in the Twenties.

After he and Annette divorced he took a job driving a delivery van. Asked to deliver some frames to the Tate one day, he decided he could make a better job than those he was carrying and became a frame designer. He designed frames for all Kyffin's exhibitions. Indeed he died the day after setting one up.

He knew everyone in London. One day he took Kyffin to a bohemian haunt Chez Kraistof on the corner of St Alban's Grove, Kensington. It had been opened by a Polish Prince Kristof Woroniecki who had come to Britain to fight with the Polish army and married a beautiful British girl to whom Kyffin was introduced. To his astonishment he discovered she was the daughter of his cousins the Williams of Parys Mountain. Her name was Julia and she told him that the last of the Parys Mountain money had gone into the restaurant. As they became more friendly she confessed, "I am not sure if I am a blood relation of yours because I do not know if Hwfa Williams was my grandfather or whether i it was the Prince of Wales. I think it more likely that it was the Prince. He was a frequent visitor to our home on Anglesey, Craig y Don. He came incognito by boat to Bangor, then down a road which is still known locally as the Prince's Drive. he was never named in conversation. He was called the Other Man."

Forty years later in 1998 still a deeply attractive woman she recalled with great fondness the young artist she met then: "He was charming but deeply combative. I think he hated authority as represented by the Arts Council. He was convinced that people were against him but I know that was not true. Everyone who met him was convinced he had a great talent."

Kyffin prized eccentrics like his Shrewsbury school fellow Sir Wynne Cemlyn-Jones of Penmaenmawr, whose portrait he painted in 1952 when he w as President of Anglesey Community Council. One day in London Sir Wynn decided to learn to drive. Eschewing an instructor, he drove on to The Mall where the traffic was less dense. To his horror, he saw the King and Queen approaching in a car from which the Royal Standard fluttered. A loyal subject he took his hand off the wheel to raise his hat. His car swerved and hit the royal car a glancing blow. Sir Wynne never drove again.

Another remarkable friend was Richard Hughes, Genius, a schoolmaster's son from Talwrn, Anglesey. Hughes had been taken up by a local landowner whom he had impressed as a schoolboy by making two hundred rabbit hutches in three days.

The landowner helped him get a scholarship to Liverpool University where he read naval architecture. Hughes qualified just as the slump hit Britain. Nothing daunted, he headed first for the South of France and then Vienna, living by drawing caricatures. He became so proficient that when he came back to Britain he drew a weekly cartoon for *Everyman* magazine. He turned down an offer to do a daily cartoon for a national daily paper because it would have been too tying. In her nineties, his widow Elrika, living in Paris and enjoying an international reputation as a maker of collages, remembered him fondly, "It was like living on a volcano. He wore a Tyrolean cape and hat, had a black beard and eyes that forever twinkled with excitement.

Hughes's greatest achievement came after the war when he became interested in water sculpture. It was he who designed the fountain which was the most talked about feature of the Festival of britain in 1951. He designed similar water features for Liverpool which still sands, for Grimsby, which was later destroyed by a council for political reasons, and his finest, for Basildon New Town, which was never built through lack of funds.

Elrika remembers Kyffin mainly for his appetite. "He was always hungry. I don't think he ate very often but Richard was a great admirer of his talent and always ready to share a meal."

Two more friends at this time were Diana Armfield R.A., R.W.S and her partner Bernard Dunston R.A. At her home in Bala, Gwynedd, Diana remembered Kyffin was a regular supper guest in the late Fifties and early Sixties:

> Our three sons, aged 5 and upwards, ate with us as a matter of course. They sat through many small dinner parties of varying interest for them, but they usually slipped away at the end of the meal to get on with their own occupations.
>
> On Kyffin evenings they seldom budged, but sat there through the general conversation to await the next anecdote from Kyffin. There might be two following hard upon each other, one employing a Welsh accent, then perhaps a gap followed by another and so it went on all through the evening. All three of them, now grown up, still ask after him.
>
> The scope of the anecdotes was wide, ranging from a near sale at a gallery, baulked when the client fell down dead as she went to sign her cheque; a battle over a tree obscuring his light; a

recurring macaroni cheese; the strange attitudes of family and friends and the outrageous behaviour of various officials in the art world. Perhaps the most relished were the ghost episodes set in Wales.

Most anecdotes tended to show him in some way as the victim, but for many years this only made the humour more vivid and his expression remained one of affectionate well being. He is, of course, the most marvellous mimic.

But as well as these wonderful flights of language we knew him as an artist deeply concerned about the state of the art world in this country. We have had many serious discussions on the topic. We also remember his loyalty to other artists and others, not necessarily artists with whom he felt sympathy.

Latterly, perhaps due to the diabetes or the epilepsy or perhaps because the official power in the art world shifted further against us, we have sometimes felt that the humour was no longer working for him as a needed safety valve, but almost increasing his suffering as he related the latest iniquities, though always in wonderful extravagant language.

We have never failed to realise that the splendid entertainment which we enjoyed did carry a grain of actual anxiety. But the telling seemed to leave him stimulated and happy. Kyffin had such a courteous strong social sense that should a guest be introduced in our circle he immediately lightened the note. What a friend to have.

Kyffin certainly had a longer dining out list than most. In his eighties the word had only to get about t hat he was not well and well upholstered ladies bearing chicken casseroles virtually queued to feed him. Some have been looking after him since his days at Highgate.

Chief among these, and loyal until his death, were three beauties Annwen Williams, Greta Williams and Valerie Price, who were known to the London Welsh as the Three Graces. So careful of his well-being were the Graces that they declined to co-operate in this biography in case it upset him; although the book was his idea.

Kyffin told me

I don't remember how I came across them. It might have been through Michael Wynn Williams who married Valerie, or it might have been through Bengy Carey Evans, Lloyd George's grandson who married Annwen.

When I met the girls they were already were engaged and living in a house in Hampstead. Annwen was a model, Greta was going to be a teacher and Val was training to be a physiotherapist. They were very beautiful and so kind. When I went over there they would rustle up a meal for me. I was always in favour of having a free meal so I saw them quite often. I painted Annwen. I was very fond of her. A hell of a lot of people were but Bengy was on the scene.

They were not only beautiful and kind but multi-talented:

Valerie Wynne Williams has been in turn since then a physiotherapist, teacher, magazine editor, TV presenter, radio interviewer, interior designer. actress, theatre director, Plaid Cymru candidate and quarry manager.

She told me in a radio interview:

I went to London as a little country girl from South Wales and was amazed to find there were more trees there than they were at home.

We were very good little girls. Annwen refused to model swim suits in case it upset people in her home village of Llanerchymedd. We were very hospitable. Kyffin often came in for a meal. The flat was on the edge of Hampstead Heath and Kyffin was teaching at Highgate so it was handy. It was a small flat. It only had two bedrooms and it was filled with his paintings. When I left to get married to Michael and help him run the family business at the Dorothea Quarry Kyffin asked me whether as a wedding present I would like him to paint my portrait or choose one of his other paintings. There was a marvellous portrait of Richard Hughes and I chose that.

Another visitor was the poet and painter David Jones. I had interviewed him and we had been in correspondence in the *Times*. We invited him to a Plaid Cymru party but he was something of a recluse and he made an excuse. However we corresponded and in time he came round. From then on he was a regular visitor. Always with the same taxi which he kept no matter how long he stayed. We tried to get him to pay it off and get another when he was ready to leave but he said he needed to have familiar things around him.

We became very close. He painted me as Aphrodite and it was shown at the Tate Gallery. I have it now with my Kyffin. My most treasured possessions.

Twice married Greta Berry recalled that the artist David Jones was obsessed with Valerie but that it was Kyffin's paintings that adorned the flat: "We had dozens of them stacked against the walls. The one I remember best was a huge mountainscape in my bedroom. It was the first thing I saw when I woke in the mornings. It was marvellous but it made me homesick. We all three of us mothered him and fed him at every possible opportunity. He didn't look as though he was eating regularly."

Rosalie Sinclair was shocked when she visited him in London; "His lodgings were always extremely modest. He had no-one to cook or clean up for him. Didn't drink, of course. In fact he kept himself very much to himself and was totally absorbed in his painting."

That was not quite true. Although the least domesticated of men, he had ways of keeping the studio clean. Years later he admitted: "I tried wherever possible to use German au pair girls as models. I discovered they had a passion for tidiness. When they came to the studio for a sitting the first thing they would do was clean it up. In those days I used to wander about a lot down by the Thames, painting. It was an odd life. William Coles, who was teaching with me, also shared my lodgings at 12 Bisham Gardens. He had plenty of money and was extremely idle. Sometimes he wouldn't get up in the morning and I had to start the lessons off. He got on terribly well with the girls. I didn't. I suppose because basically I am a melancholic. I am seldom happy but I hide it by being a clown."

Curiously none of the girls with whom Kyffin claimed he was in love as a young man realised it. Interviewed as old ladies they almost all affected surprise when they were told how he felt. It could be, of course, an accomplished act on their part. Or perhaps Kyffin's courting techniques were so elliptical as to be invisible. That was certainly not true of Coles, almost a caricature, perhaps knowingly, as so many art students were in the Forties, of the painter Strickland in Somerset Maugham's novel *The Moon and Sixpence*.

In his second volume of autobiography, *A Wider Sky*, discreetly altering his name, Kyffin told how Coles had visited Frank Welby, another artist and mutual friend in Paris. When he arrived at his flat the door had been opened by Welby's mistress, a voluptuous milliner called Suzy. She told him that Welby was visiting England. By the time he returned Coles had replaced him in Suzy's bed. Astonishingly Welby accepted the situation. He made up a bed in the kitchen and became both cuckold and cook.

Coles was capable of even greater treachery as Kyffin wrote:

> Suzy discovered she was pregnant ... he realised that for the first time in his life he was not in control of a situation and his money could not buy his way out. He returned to Torquay where his father agreed to stop his allowance so that Suzy could not benefit from the family wealth. Many were the times Suzy telephoned me from Paris. Many times she was in tears as she cried over the telephone "I hate him. I hate him. But oh what a lover".

Welby offered to mary Suzy and adopt Coles's baby but she refused. Kyffin was clearly shocked by his friend. He admitted:

> I saw little of Coles when he returned. He said I must never mention about Suzy in Paris. I tried to get in touch with him several times when I was writing *A Wider Sky* but I didn't get a reply so I assumed he was dead. Then at my show in the Thackeray in 1998 there was an entry in the Remarks Book. It read 'I am William Coles's sister'.
>
> The trouble with Coles was that he had this immense talent and he taught me more than anyone ever did. But he had no stamina, no strength to see a picture through. I thought it was laziness but I think now it was his heart.
>
> He was one of those absolutely brilliant people who die unknown. He taught me to look at everything. To work out the colour of a puddle,what colour the sun was, shining on a wet roof. He told me everything is colour. He drew beautifully but he just had not got the stamina.
>
> He used to come and stay at home. My mother couldn't stand him because he wouldn't lift a finger. He was totally self absorbed.

Although he would never admit it, painting talent was not the only attribute of his friend that Kyffin envied. There was his success with girls: "He was so arrogant and the girls worshiped him for it. In our lodgings he was always being rung up by girls who had fallen in love with him. I remember one literally going mad on the phone. She insisted he was there when he wasn't. She got more and more agitated until I put the phone down. She was found wandering on Hampstead Heath and incarcerated in Coney Hatch. It must have been very provoking for Kyffin whose own love life was constantly being ship wrecked:

> In life drawing classes at the Slade we had a new pose every month and you had to draw lots for an easel. Coles never used to come in time for the draw. He would stroll in at half past ten because he knew that lots of girls would offer him their easels. He would never even say thank you. I remember when another friend at the Slade Tom Griffiths, Coles and I stayed in Ffestiniog where he painted lots of lovely paintings. Then he went off to Paris and faded out of our lives. William never had an exhibition, though he was streets ahead. and in a different class altogether. But he wasn't totally obsessed and without that it doesn't work
>
> We went to the Scilly Isles on a painting holiday and he didn't paint a single picture. I sent him a limerick:

> There was a young artist called Willy
> Went to paint in the Island of Scilly
> He thought it more fun
> just to lie in the sun
> So the output of Willy was nilly.

Six

Slowly Kyffin's pictures began to sell but there were still disastrous interludes. In the late forties he was asked to have an exhibition in Terry Hebberd's gallery in a music shop in Caernarfon. A Blaenau Ffestiniog woman saw a painting she liked. She asked the price and when Hebberd told her £60 she said "I cannot afford that but I must have it". She sat down and had just started to write a cheque when she dropped dead, to be reborn as an after dinner anecdote. The excitement of spending so much on a picture had been too much for her. On another occasion in a gallery in the National Museum of Wales, Kyffin noticed with horror that someone had got out a biro and scribbled all over one of his pictures. His was the only picture in the gallery that had not been glazed.

He entered the competition to mark the fiftieth anniversary of the Football Association. The entries, paintings of footballers, were to be exhibited in Londonderry House, Park Lane. Kyffin entered a painting of one of his Highgate schoolboys in his house colours. Although it did not win a prize it was bought by the Contemporary Art Society and presented to the Glynn Vivian Art Gallery in Swansea. Subsequently the director wrote that he had loaned the picture to a local mental home where a woman inmate had attacked the picture with a knife and severed the head from the body. Would Kyffin restore it if he had the canvas relined? Kyffin painted in a new head. His bill read "To restoring a footballer's head. £120. To repairing footballers shorts £50."

Mrs Nancy Thomas of Aberaeron bought an inoffensive painting of cottages at Llanddona. Kyffin tells the story:

> One day I was in the studio and I got a call. A voice said my name is Annie Williams. I am speaking on behalf of Mrs Nancy

Thomas. A terrible thing has happened. Her husband came home from work and saw your painting on the wall. And pulled out a revolver and shot himself dead in front of it. And the picture is covered in blood. Will you take the blood off?

In time I got the reputation of being the most lethal painter in Britain. Also my pictures were stolen all over the place. I had a very big picture, thirty inches by fifty, of Harlech which was stolen from the common room in UCW Swansea. Thirty were stolen from my studio without me knowing it. Not surprising. I had 500 at the times.

In 1980 there was a retrospective exhibition of privately owned paintings by Kyffin. A few weeks after they were returned a letter came from a Lady Robinson in Northampton accusing the organisers of damaging a work which she had loaned. The organisers contacted Kyffin who offered to collect the painting and make it right free of charge. The organisers were amazed at her solicitor's reply. They wrote "Our client wants it done professionally".

Apart from part time teaching and intermittent sales, his other source of income was buying and selling pictures. His mother hit the roof when he paid £14 for a picture he believed to be a Richard Wilson at a junk shop in Chester. No-one in London would accept his attribution. Kyffin knew he was right and took it to William Constable, the director of the Boston Museum of Fine Arts, who had just written the definitive work on Wilson. Constable recognised it at once. "Ah, the missing Wilson," he said. "I was looking for it for my book." He wrote about it in the *Burlington Magazine* and a dealer snapped it up.

Other paintings he had to sell included those he had inherited from his cousins, the Ramsays, including a fine Marco Ricci which now resides in a major collection in Italy.

Although it had upset Rosalie Sinclair, a certain amount of squalor is to be expected at the lodgings of an up and coming young artist. Despite the ministrations of German au pairs Kyffin's home in Bisham Gardens exceeded the permissible amount by a wide margin. The green hall, the dirt encrusted paintings, even the dung brown painted woodwork could be overlooked. Not so the smells. Part cat part dog, part cabbage, they merged into the overwhelming odour of his landlady Miss Mary

Josling's stockpot, which was forever abubble. It was the stockpot that finally drove him in a desperate search for a new home.

It was only then, he later insisted, that he began to take himself seriously as a painter: "It was only when I had nowhere to paint that I realised how hooked I had become. I was going round knocking on doors to find a studio but they were all occupied by old women who weren't painters. It made me very angry. I just carried on painting. Goodness knows why. No-one liked my work."

Leila Troup offered to help. She had a friend Jean Brett married to a diplomat Norman Merriway, both of whom Kyffin knew. When Merriway was *en poste* in Rome he had holidayed with them at the Embassy In London they came to his rescue with the offer of a room in their basement in St John's Wood.

Kyffin quickly moved in and just as quickly regretted it.

> I was the sort of dogsbody. I had to pay my rent, I had to stoke the boiler, I had to mow the lawn, I had to trim the vine, I had to babysit, I had to produce pictures for their house, I had to clear the children's toffee papers.
>
> I was at their beck and call, their tame artist and still they complained.
>
> I think the trouble was that I did not pay enough attention to Jean and I think she resented it. She was very pretty and she liked men to flutter around. But I was a friend of her friend and it would have been quite wrong to dance attendance.
>
> She suddenly started hating me. I had never been really hated before. Every time she spoke to me her face became creased. They did everything they could to get me to go. Once I was ordered up to their living room. She was knitting. Her husband told me to sit down. He had been given orders, I think. He was a nice chap basically. He said, "Now Taff, you haven't been pulling your weight you know." I went through the list. He shook his head. "You haven't been picking up many toffee papers in the yard and we have all got to pull our weight. If I had been in your place I know I would have been an A1 tenant. I am afraid you only add up to a Beta minus."
>
> The final row brought everything to a head. I got a note from Jean to say that I had insulted their daily. The daily was unaware of this when I asked her. But in the end I did go. I had to put all my pictures into a basement at school and move in with another painter, Fred Uhlman and his wife.

When I wrote *Across the Straits* I felt it was too smug so I put in a bit about these people although I changed the name.

About five years after the book had come out I got a letter from Jean Brett saying how appaled she was to read the book. She was so angry she said, "Take immediate steps to remove all the paintings you gave us when you lived in the house. Including a life sized portrait of their son. I could have sent in a bill for the painting for about £15,000 but I just burned the letter. He became the Ambassador to Poland.

Fred Uhlman was German by birth. When war broke out he was interned in the Isle of Man. He shared a house with two eccentrics. One, a professor of pure mathematics, believed he was a dachshund. The other, the Dadaist Kurt Schwitters, believed he was an Alsatian. Occasionally they would meet on the landing and bark at each other.

Kyffin painted Uhlman and presented the portrait to the National Library. Later in Wales their friendship grew. Though Uhlman, when he began to make a name, used Kyffin – whom he always called Coffin – unscrupulously. Kyffin relates, "He used to ring me up occasionally and say 'Coffin my dear. Can you bring me some of your drawings of Wales. I wish to do some paintings of Wales.' I would bring him down a dozen drawings and he would copy them and sell them for quite a lot of money. I couldn't make any money at all. In fact one of his paintings of a windmill at Llanerchymedd which he did from a drawing of mine is the national collection. Kyffin did not mind this ruthless But he was extremely cross to read a *Daily Telegraph* review of an early exhibition with Fred Uhlman and Jonah Jones in Port Meirion. It read: "Williams has been doing some paintings in Uhlman country."

After Uhlman moved to Croft Castle, where he was to spend the rest of his life, they saw less of each other. So little indeed that Uhlman once wrote to ask if Kyffin was dead. In reply Kyffin sent off one of his impromptu rhymes:

A man from Penrhyndeudraeth said
That Manfred fred was dead
No indeed he is not I said
He has merely gone right off his head
And taken to his bed
In the Croft Castle Potting Shed

Sadly it Uhlman who died six months later.

In the four days each week he had free, Kyffin tried to paint two pictures. This at a time when he could hardly afford paint and in addition was deeply worried at the deteriorating mental state of his mother:

> I came home one Christmas and found her in a terrible state..
> She had all the family silver out. She insisted some had been
> stolen and all night she moaned and went on counting and
> counting each piece. I could do nothing with her.
>
> She gradually got worse and worse until the doctor came and
> said she would have to go to a mental home. He begged me not
> to get Dick back because he knew she liked Dick and in these
> cases people tend to destroy the thing they love most. So we had
> to keep Dick out of it. Finally they came to take her away and it
> was terrible. She broke away and ran down the lane with these
> people hunting after her. They caught her in a rick yard. It was
> absolute hell. I was there for a whole week trying to help. In the
> end I had to send for Dick. We thought the only thing to do was
> to buy a small house for her on Anglesey and she went there.
>
> We used to come home and she was still very protective of
> Dick. There was this business of his holiday abroad. She was
> contemptuous of the suggestion. "How can he go abroad with
> no-one to look after him?"
>
> I said "I'll go abroad."
>
> And she said "It is different for you."
>
> I didn't point out that I was an epileptic but there was nothing
> wrong with him.
>
> In the end I said to him, "Look tell me where you want to go
> and I will take you. He said he would like to go to Scotland. The
> further north we got the more insecure he got, worrying where
> he would be sleeping that night. He became very strange. We got
> to Ullapool and he just completely flipped. I knew I had to get
> him back to Chester.
>
> The next year I took him to Ireland to stay with one of my
> pupils. We had no sooner got there than a telegram came from
> my mother saying she was in hospital with a broken arm and
> wanted us home. So we had to pack up. We got home and found
> she hadn't broken her arm. She just wanted to see him.
>
> By this time he was getting not to like her. It ended by her
> suddenly realising towards the end of her life that I actually cared
> for her more than he did. This was a terrible blow for her. When
> she was living in Gadlys, the house we got for her, she used to go
> out at night and sleep under the hedges. She would turn up at

Treffos, the old family home, the next morning covered in leaves and twigs. She was very unhappy. We are an extraordinary family. I have never known what it is to be happy. But I am better off than she was. She thought all her apprehensions were valid. I always question mine.

She desperately didn't want to be a burden but her apprehension was a terrible strain. I sensed she thought she was inferior. She was always terribly worried what people thought about her. She used to get furious because I wanted to paint on Sundays. I was about forty at the time.

Outside his family people were beginning to appreciate his work. In 1946 his first picture was accepted by the Royal Academy. He had less success when he tried to get dealers interested in his work. He was astonished how rude they were and the insulting things they said. One gallery owner described him as a poor imitator of Cezanne, another claimed he was far too like Camille Pissarro. Another gallery owner said, "For God's sake hide them. Someone may come in."

The only good mannered reception he got was from Colonel Beddington in Wildenstein's. Kyffin recalled: "His real name was Moses. When he joined the cavalry he thought it wiser to change his name. The first morning he went into the officers' mess under his new name there was a huge notice which read 'The Lord said unto Moses, Good morning Mr Beddington.'

He was very nice. He said, "Now then Mr Williams I am going to pay you a compliment and compare your work with Daumier." He sent a lackey to fetch a Daumier and compared us. Otherwise everywhere I went I got a flea in my ear. Fortunately my reports at Shrewsbury had ben so uniformly awful I had learned to put up with such treatment. When the critics have been rude I have not been too depressed. It was just like school. When I started looking for galleries in 1946 I quickly realised no-one can ever get a gallery in the West End without influence and I had none.

Writing of Kyffin's life it is tempting to see a guiding hand gently pushing him, not always willingly, to his present eminence as the greatest Welsh artist. As a boy out hunting he met Ernest Naish who taught him to paint. No sooner had an army doctor started him thinking about becoming an artist than he met

Gwyneth the lovely landgirl who got him into the Slade. At Highgate School a sympathetic headmaster allowed him to work part time and paint the rest of the week. Soon the guiding hand was to propel into his path the man who was to launch him on his career: Ralph Edwards.

Modern Wales can be divided into two periods, Before and After Saunders Lewis. That Liverpool-born Welsh minister's son moved to Paris in the Twenties where he fell in with the expatriate Irish community. He complained to Synge, the playwright, that he could find no subject for his Muse. Synge advised him to go home and write about the Welsh struggle for freedom. "But they aren't struggling," objected Lewis. "Then go home and start a struggle." Lewis took Synge's advice and virtually single handedly invented Welsh Nationalism. In the Sixties he made an inflammatory broadcast on BBC Wales calling on the young men of Wales to rise and shake off their oppressors. A new Wales had been born.

Until then Wales had been ruled unofficially by the London Welsh, among whom Ralph Edwards reigned supreme. A farmer's son from South Wales, he was an irascible little man, plagued with a painful ulcer. But he was a polymath and still, long after his death, he is recognised as the greatest expert on English furniture in the world. He was the author of the standard work on the subject.

Edwards met Kyffin on the recommendation of Professor Schwabe, whom he had asked about young Welsh artists of promise. He liked what he saw at the artist's studio and bought two pictures, one for himself and one for the Contemporary Art Society of Wales for which he was a talent spotter. He also recommended the young unknown to his friends. Amongst them Captain Geoffrey Crawshay, a giant of a man bought two pictures and invited Kyffin to his annual grouse shoot on the slopes of Plynlimmon. It was not so much a shoot as an annual gathering of Welshmen from all walks of life and considerable eminence who between them controlled Wales. The original Taffia.

Geoffrey Crawshay was, in his heyday, one of the finest shots in Britain. The same could not be said for some of his guests, who included architects, policemen, bards, judges and servicemen, but their power was considerable. One day Kyffin and two other guns who comprised the 'shoot art committee' were in a car driven by a local known for obvious reasons as Duodenal Jenkins. It was the sort of day Kyffin always hoped for, grey and misty, when shooting was abandoned and the arts set could drive to Gregynog to see the remarkable collection of art there, owned by two spinster sisters Gwendoline and Margaret Davies. The paintings were mostly French impressionists. Monet, Pissarro, Cezanne, Gauguin and Renoir, plus Van Gogh. There was sculpture by Rodin and other paintings by John, Sickert and many more.

As they anticipated the joys to come the talk turned to the future of the collection, The arts set decided that when the sisters died their collection must go to the National Museum of Wales, although there was strong interest from other UK Galleries. The paintings are now housed in their own magnificent wing of the National Gallery of Wales.

Ralph Edwards' son is Lord Crickhowell, the former Welsh Secretary Nicholas Edwards. At the family home in the Black Mountains he told me:

> My father and mother lived on Chiswick Mall when Kyffin was teaching at Highgate. They all used to go up to this extraordinary shoot. There was a teetotal hotel in Llandinam. It was owned by Lord Davies who abominated liquor in any form. Lord Davies even controlled the time the local people went to bed by switching off the electrical supply to the whole village.
>
> The shoot was an annual event at which the social chit chat was about Wales, its politics and art. It was a great deal more important than the shooting. Geoffrey [Crawshay] had been a very great shot. He once told me in his heyday he was one of the dozen best shots in the country he would shoot fifty thousand cartridges a year. But he was very badly injured in the First World War. He couldn't bend his right arm. He had a special gun made which he threw up with his left hand and he was still able to out-shoot most people.

His guests at the annual shoot to which Kyffin was invited were all prominent people in Welsh life, involved in the National Museum and such matters. It did Kyffin no harm to know them. Among the people Kyffin met on the shoot were Sir Wynne Cemlyn-Jones, Sir Wynn Weldon and his son Huw (who was to rise to eminence in the BBC) and the Rev Twm Hollingworth, an East End vicar with a wonderful voice. Crawshay took over the teetotal hotel – the Red Lion – and for the duration of the shoot it flowed with beer and every evening there was a sing-song round the piano.

One of the most important meetings was with a Director of the National Museum and Gallery of Wales, Sir Leonard Twiston Davies, whose son Tony later held the same position. But it was to his teenage daughter Suzanne that Kyffin became closest. Now Suzanne Hunter is an international journalist. At her home in the Bahamas she remembered that in London and for many years Kyffin kept his epilepsy quiet.

> He used to take me out to dinner (in a very platonic way – he was always falling in love with people whose portraits he had painted, but never wanted to marry so far as I know) and I thought it odd that he would ring up sometimes and say "I cannot take you out to dinner to-morrow. I think I am going to have 'flu". I used to think, why don't you wait until you have actually got 'flu. But later I discovered that he could feel the epilepsy coming on, and naturally, didn't want to give me a shock.
>
> I was working for the BBC and the BBC medic Dr Elizabeth Fletcher had a Kyffin on her wall. It turned out that Kyffin had lodged with her. She told me about the epilepsy though Kyffin was later to be open about it.
>
> When he did take me out to dinner he would frighten me to death by collecting me in this large van, big enough to hold his landscapes. I was frightened because it had a rear engine and it appeared as though there was nothing between us and the bus ahead.
>
> He was a terrific companion. Very amusing. Very funny about Highgate School. When required to do a portrait of Guy Fawkes, the boys always did an exact picture of Kyffin complete with drooping moustaches. He was always having rows with his headmaster who wanted the boys to learn to paint. He reckoned they did not need to learn to draw but Kyffin was adamant.
>
> He was pretty critical of various presidents of the National Museum, but luckily much admired my brother Tony and Tim Edwards, Ralph's son. He used to say least least they know about art.
>
> I think he quarrelled with most of the members of most of the committees he was on and certainly had no time for most RAs.
>
> He worried terribly about his brother Dick. He used to

despair when they were going on holiday. He would tell me they would reach a likely hotel and Kyffin would suggest they see if it had rooms.

Dick usually replied, "But it would be so humiliating if they haven't got rooms and turn us away. Don't let's go in." He said they often ended up sleeping in the car.

Lord Crickhowell remembered Suzanne and Kyffin as a devoted couple but admitted Kyffin fell in love with many women in his life. As a schoolboy, he recalled Kyffin's many visits to the family home:

> Kyffin became a regular visitor to our home where there was a very great ritual of tea. My father suffered all his life from a duodenal ulcer. His temper only improved after tea about four in the afternoon. Cake and jam and everything. To say that Kyffin came every week would be to exaggerate but he came very often to tea and supper. He became a close friend of mine when I was a schoolboy at Westminster and of my brother Tim. He was always very welcome. He was full of wonderful tales and we were enchanted by them. Kyffin wore venerable corduroy trousers and an artist's jacket and his moustache was even longer.
>
> We had a pestilential Jack Russell terrier who once ate the shoulder out of a chinchilla coat of an extremely rich American visitor. On one occasion he was tugging round Kyffin's leg. When he got up from the table he found the whole of his corduroy trousers to the knee had virtually disappeared.

The benefits of acquaintance with the family far outweighed the sartorial hazards:

> One day my father, who was on the Council and Court of the National Museum for fifty years, said "Look here, Kyffin. Its time you had a show." He was also a buyer s for the Contemporary Art Society of Wales and very much in the way of encouraging young artists. He persuaded Byam Shaw the senior partner at Colnaghi and Co., to put an exhibition by Kyffin in the gallery. It was rather an unusual show for Colnaghi who specialised in old master prints and drawings but nevertheless Kyffin had his first one man show at Colnaghi, in Bond Street.

Kyffin recalled with gratitude how Shaw and another dealer called Tom Baskett came to see his work. In all the gallery put on three of his shows including one of his drawings which he shared with Augustus John and Muirhead Bone. Although his relations with Colnaghi were harmonious they would never show his portraits. Once again Ralph Edwards used his influence to put Kyffin in touch with the Leicester Galleries, which agreed to put him in a show with two young, fashionable artists Anthony Fry and Ronald Searle. A friend warned him that the art world was behind them and they would be praised at his expense. And so it proved.

Eric Newton, whom Kyffin believed to be the best art critic in London, wrote: "Mr Fry at thirty is a more sensitive artist than Mr Williams at forty, whose ponderous unimaginative and insensitive works are shown in the adjoining gallery." Neville Wallace wrote in the *Observer* "What bad luck for the steady-going Mr Williams to be sandwiched between the genius of Mr Fry and Mr Searle."

The most cruel of all the critics was Nigel Gosling who wrote three words in the *Sunday Times*: "Herman and Soda." He implied that Kyffin was a pale imitation of Joseph Herman.

It is said that artists are not affected by their critics. Strange, then, that forty years later Kyffin could quote all three verbatim. He was most upset by Gosling's cruel jibe. At that time he had never seen Herman's work and still insisted to his dying day that the only thing they had in common was that they both painted with black ink.

There were more perceptive critics. In the *Liverpool Daily Post* Elizabeth Coxhead wrote after visiting one of his thirty one-man exhibitions:

> His work is not much bought by the public and he is forced to eke out the money he gets from his paintings by working as a schoolmaster. He says ruefully "I don't paint what people want.
> The fact is that like all artists of original vision he is having a long struggle to impose it.... His recognition will come not from fashionable people who want something modish to hang on their walls but from climbers and walkers who know the hills as Kyffin knows them.

How true that turned out to be.

SIX

Kyffin insisted until the end of his life that the Arts Council and the Welsh Arts establishment hated him and his work. It was true that in later life there were some pretty spectacular quarrels. Lord Crickhowell opines: "I think he was probably right in thinking – if there is such a thing as an Arts Establishment – it was against him. The reason was, of course, that he expressed himself strongly. He painted in a traditional style and had very strong views of things that have gone on in the art schools in this country for forty years. With some justice. He was almost intemperate, but absolutely right. Even those students who want to be abstract painters need the basic skills of draughtsmen. My niece, whom he encouraged very much, went to the Ecole des Beaux Arts in Paris. Students there are not allowed to do anything for three years but draw and draw and draw. She only painted after she left."

It was those strong views which led to disagreements with the Welsh Arts Council. No-one knows more about those disagreements than Llion Williams the former Director of the North Wales Arts Association. Llion met Kyffin formally when he was appointed in 1974. but he had known the painter vaguely in London when Lion was a science teacher in the late Fifties.

In those days he sold very little. But he was a great teacher. You only have to look at the list of successful painters he taught. Yet he was never asked to teach in an art school.

A year after I joined the Association we got the idea of doing an exhibition of crow-stepped gabled houses in North Wales to mark European Architectural year. We set up a set and invited Kyffin, who was interested in architecture as art, to act as chairman. We opened it at the National Eisteddfod in Criccieth and I told Kyffin he would have to make the opening speech. He was reluctant because he would have to speak in Welsh and he did not think he was sufficiently fluent.

I insisted because I knew that was an excuse. When he went out painting he spoke in Welsh to farmers, and he performed with great success. Nine months later he came into my office in Bangor and said did you know there was an art gallery in Llandudno? I didn't. But I looked and there it was. A custom built art gallery which was rented to Rushworth's Music Shop who were using it as a warehouse. I knew it had possibilities but Kyffin wanted it for the Royal Cambrian Academy, of which he was president, so I held back.

I was delighted when the RCA refused to move there. I brought a gathering together to look at it and we got working. We set up a council of management and a limited company with charitable status. I was in Cardiff one day and Aneurin Thomas and Peter Jones collared me. "I hear you are going to put Kyffin on the council of management,"one of them said. I replied, "Of course, why shouldn't I?"

They said "He is a danger to Welsh art, that man. A bad influence on art in Wales".

I said "You are entitled to your opinion but we cannot leave Kyffin out of the development of a major gallery in North Wales."

I just ignored them.

In the event we ran into financial difficulties. It was going to cost £250,000 to renovate the building and we were fifty thousand short. The only source of funds was the buildings set of the Arts Council. We soon sensed that we would only get help if we got rid of Kyffin. In the end we called their bluff. We went to Cardiff to tell them we couldn't afford to complete the contract. We told them that if they refused help we would hand over the lease to the Arts Council and they would have to run it. They realised the political implications. I had already told a lot of people of influence that the Arts Council wanted to run it from Cardiff. That was anathema. So they gave in and gave us the money.

Our plan for the gallery was to have a balanced programme. We were prepared to push to the frontiers of art with difficult exhibitions so long as the balance was maintained. But that didn't happen.

With his enormous knowledge of art Kyffin was in a position of strength. But Kyffin, Leslie Jones and myself were accused of keeping the gallery back. We resigned.

Fifteen years ago we put together a retrospective of Kyffin's work. It took us two years to get it off the ground. There was

resistance and ninety-nine per cent of the works are in private
hands so insurance was a great problem. The National Museum
is the only gallery in Wales which has a government indemnity so
we had to get them on board. Finally they agreed and the exhibition had a critical success.

The National Museum wanted us to launch it in Turner
House but we pointed out that the exhibition was the work of a
major artist and it should start in the National Gallery. Until they
opened a gallery of Welsh art – another Kyffin suggestion – he
was represented in the gallery with a hopeless example of his
work from the late Forties. He offered two canvasses to replace it
free of charge, but they weren't interested. They even hung one
of his paintings in the new refectory.

A subsequent director, Colin Ford, was for accepting and a
painting for the gallery was kept at Oriel Ynys Mon but it was
never collected. Somewhere in middle management he had an
enemy. I do not understand it. Kyffin put himself in every
picture. There are other Welsh painters who are fine craftsmen;
but they do not seem to love their subjects in the way Kyffin did.
He used unusual colours and used them with great subtlety

He was never interested in money. His prices were lower than
most. For a good Kyffin oil you paid around £5,000 in Sothebys
which is chicken feed because there will only ever be one Kyffin.
People loved him and will buy his works.

I remember telling Aneurin Thomas, who was Chairman of
the Welsh Arts Council, that his Council was scared Kyffin would
start a Welsh school of painting and that would be anathema to
the Arts Council because it was promoting the 56 Group in
South Wales. Their paintings could have come from anywhere.
When you look at a Scottish group there is a Scottish stamp on
their work. Apart from Kyffin, there has never been that national
stamp on our painting. I said the last thing the Council wants is
a Welsh school of art. He didn't deny it. This reaction against
Kyffin manifests itself in some strange ways. In 1997, when he
was asked to do a master class on TV, there was not an art school
which would let its pupils take part.

Williams believes that in his day the Council in Wales didn't
like successful artists. "They were running a social service for
struggling artists. When Lady Anglesey became Chairman of the
Arts Council, the Director and Peter Jones the Art Director
immediately concluded he would influence her because they were
friends. Anything to do with art she would be seeking Kyffin's
opinion. It was nonsense, of course. She is her own woman with

Dear Ian and Celia
many thanks for
the Memoirs
of →

See you on the 16th
ever thine

Kittin (van) Williams

Many thanks. I will be
at Abersvaint on
Sunday 21st May

Kyffin O Fôn

SKID MAWR O FÔN

Come back soon

very strong views and opinions but they were paranoid.
Williams pointed out that Kyffin was never asked to take part
in any overseas exhibition.

> The art establishment, and I would include in that the National
> Museum and Art Gallery, never missed an opportunity to stab
> him in the back. He was put on the Art Committee but he was a
> thorn in their side. He would question their purchases. I reckon
> Kyffin was one of the best art historians in Wales. He was so well
> versed in art history he could constructively criticise modern art
> and show where it had gone wrong. Twenty years ago I commis-
> sioned him to give the Ben Bowen Annual Lecture, 'Is tradition
> in danger?' It was a cracking speech. He infuriated the establish-
> ment because, quite rightly, he criticised all the isms.
>
> I forget who described art as a passionate mistress but Kyffin
> committed himself wholeheartedly to her. In his eightieth year he
> showed me a painting he had done with Crib Coch in the
> foreground with Snowdon in the distance. It was one of his best.
> How did he do it?
>
> That year he had fifty oils in a London exhibition and another
> fifty in Swansea. He had done an oil of R.S. Thomas which
> caught the spirit of the man to a T. Quite his best portrait. At
> eighty. It is an incredible talent.

In fact the talent was recognised a good deal earlier than Kyffin
chose to admit. He was one of three Slade students who were
chosen as promising students and exhibited in the Ashmolean.

Early in his career it was a view which the Arts Council of
Wales clearly shared. In 1949 the Council bought a painting and
wrote glowingly of its purchase: "To know him casually one
would hardly believe the fire which burns in him, a fire which
seems to be nourished equally by a love of the mountains and a
love of art. His gift is rather in his sensitivity and imaginative use
of tonal arrangement rather than in precise drawing."

Llion Williams believes Kyffin's reputation was also bound into
his nationality:

> I don't think he had quite such a following outside Wales because
> the English don't understand us or even recognise we exist. They
> probably don't recognise the mood that Kyffin expresses
> whereas Welshmen can hardly wait for the next show. There is
> no-one capable of painting the mood that is Wales better than he.
>
> He did paint the atmosphere of his native land extraordinarily

well. The contrasts of light, the sometimes very sombre mood. Even the way he applied his paint was Welsh. He put on paint the way rocks look.

Then of course there were the Kyffin people. Wherever we travelled round Wales with my children they would always point outside the car and say "Look, there is a Kyffin man" or a "Kyffin dog". They are umistakeably characteristic of Wales.

And of course his portraits are wonderful. I was very sad when he ceased to paint them. My brother Tim was Director of the National Museum of Wales. After he died Kyffin was asked if he would paint his portrait. He had given up portraits but Tim was such a friend he said he would try. He had to paint from photographs but tore up the result because he said he could not do Tim justice. It's not so much the great people he has done as the country people and the children. They are remarkable.

In 1949 Kyffin painted the portrait of Sir Leonard Twiston-Davies, then director of the National Museum of Wales. His daughter Sue recalls

Dad hated it. He said it made him look like a Welsh mountain. He refused to allow it to be hung and I believe it is still skulking in a cellar there. To compensate Dad, Kyffin gave him a lovely black and white water colour of the Appian Way which he had just painted. Nevertheless in the Arts Council exhibition that year there were three Kyffin portraits, though the catalogue goes on to say "One feels that portraiture is a professional activity whereas painting the mountains of Gwynedd almost a religion."

I think that, apart from the landscapes, some of his best pictures are of horses – stout cobs with farmers – both Welsh and Patagonian – trotting along in a purposeful way. Also of Welsh collies frozen to the ground, stalking the sheep. I have never seen a painter who can get so well the feeling of suspended action, that the dog is about to fly through the air after the flock.

I also treasure a cartoon he did for me. 'Stout Cortez standing on a peak in Darien' – the peak in question was one of my mother's pekinese.

Kyffin certainly preferred painting landscapes. He gave up the business of painting portraits with considerable relief.

He wrote of the North Wales landscape in an article a few years later: "An artist can live in North Wales all his life and feel at the end of it he has not completed his work." A little later in another magazine he wrote that the great era of portrait painting was over.

"Portrait painting as a great art has suffered and is now nearly extinct. Art historians of the future may say portraiture began in Western Europe with Van Dyck and ended with Kokoschka. Today the portrait painter tends to use the head as an object to show the agony of our time or to work out clinically an effect of light."

Kyffin certainly changed that. He would have none of the notion that an artist paints character. He wrote: "The job of getting a likeness is difficult enough on its own. The painter in the development of the portrait changes the character unintentionally all of the time. A flick of the brush and conceit can be turned into humility, the stroke of a palette knife and strength can be turned to weakness. The character can change maybe three hundred times until finally the artist sees a look in his portrait and says 'That is it'."

The Arts Council did not ignore him completely. In 1952 it bought his portrait of Tom Owens which was exhibited at the National Eisteddfod. And in the foreword to a booklet the Council published on Welsh art is this praise, "Kyffin Williams has so made the turbulent mountains of North Wales his subject he might almost be called the Painter of Gwynedd."

In 1953 a painting of Cader Idris was part of an exhibition organised by what was then the Welsh set of the Arts Council of Great Britain. In 1956, after a similar exhibition, the *Times* criticised Augustus John's work as flash but said of Kyffin: "His is one of the two most attractive paintings in the room".

Indeed the collection of cuttings from newspapers in the Fifties which are held in the archives of Oriel Ynys Môn are full of praise for his work. The archive also contains a catalogue of a 1957 exhibition in Porthmadog Art Club, where Kyffin's works were the cheapest in the show. A buyer could have picked up one of his paintings for £7 and the dearest was £50. A year later at the Tegfryn Art Gallery in Menai Bridge, Ynys Mon, the price had jumped to £200.

The Tegfryn, which still flourishes, had a strange genesis. Its owner Gwen Brown wanted to raise funds so that the ATC squadron her husband commanded in Menai Bridge could buy a link trainer. She hit on the idea of a painting sale in her house and Kyffin was one of the local artists who contributed. The sale was such a success she decided to open a gallery. That gallery the Tegfryn became one of the most successful in Wales. But Kyffin remembered that one of his paintings in that first exhibition was a nude and Mrs Brown was so embarrassed she hid it behind the kitchen door.

It was in her gallery that Mrs Brown encountered the unluckiest art thief in history. She was having coffee with Kyffin when a man walked in with a pile of paintings under his arm. "Want to buy a painting?" he asked. Mrs Brown saw they were five paintings stolen Kyffin's studio in London. She called Kyffin down and the thief shot out, leaving his loot behind.

At his next exhibition, a year after the Tegfryn show, at the Thackeray Gallery in London the cheapest painting was £325 and the dearest an astronomical (for those days) £575. One of Kyffin's most successful exhibitions in London came in 1970 when P and D Colnaghi showed his 'Drawings from Patagonia'. It might be argued that it was this exhibition which brought him to a wider audience. Within four years he was to become a Royal Academician; indeed for many years he was the only Welsh RA. By 1997 he had paintings in the collections of the Arts Council of Great Britain, the National Library and the National Museum of Wales, the Walker Art Gallery in Liverpool, the Royal Academy, Swansea, Newport, Hereford, Coventry and the collections of many education committees all over Britain.

Typically Kyffin always maintained his most successful painting was of a cock pheasant. It combined his love of nature, hunting and art. He explained, "I painted it, shot it, ate it and sold it."

SEVEN

The Patagonian drawings were the fruit of a Winston Churchill scholarship to visit the country which he had won in 1968. Only a Welshman can appreciate the call that Patagonia has on the hearts of his countrymen. To an outsider the story of the trusting farm workers and their families who were persuaded in 1865 to leave their homeland with promises of a golden land in South America only to find inhospitable desert is one of cruel exploitation. Welshmen take pride in the way their ancestors irrigated the desert, conquered the hearts of the natives and found prosperity. The sad irony is that, in the Falklands War in 1983, Trelew in Patagonia was the biggest base for the Argentinian Air Force which bombed the ship bringing the Welsh Guards to battle. The survivors unkowingly fought Patagonian Welshmen who had been conscripted into the war.

A thousand miles south west from Buenos Aires, the Chubut river breaks out from the Andes and carves through the sterile plateau of the Patagonian desert to the Atlantic four hundred miles to the west. Forty four miles from the sea the river valley extends into a flat land between four and five miles wide. It was here in a dry, windblasted and salt sodden desert that 150 Welshmen, women and children settled to make a new Wales.

On 25 July 1865 the tea clipper Mimosa from Liverpool had deposited them to bitter winter storms. There were no houses, not even huts. They carved holes in the cliffs for shelter. Cattle had been driven down by two of the party who had gone ahead. Pushing their herd before them, they crossed forty miles of desert before they reached the valley of the Chubut where they made their first settlement.

The Indians who were at constant war with Argentina were set to massacre the interlopers. They were won over by the gentle ways of the Welsh and their voices as they sang in the chapel which was one of the first buildings they erected. They became friends and allies in the struggle for existence of the first pioneering years. The Indians taught the Welsh to hunt the ostrich and the llama. The Welsh taught the Indians to bake bread. Even the Argentine government, delighted that their desert lands were being settled and the Indians pacified, helped with the supply of stock. At first the crops were poisoned by the deep lying salt in the land. Floods washed away their seed and the harsh sun killed the early shoots. The Welsh, fine farmers, washed it out with gentle irrigation canals. Altogether they dug two hundred miles of canal.

Within twenty years the land had been divided into districts with names like Bethesda, each with its own chapel. The crops were growing and the desert was tamed. The Indians told their Welsh friends of a beautiful green valley at the foot of the Andes that had no need of irrigation. One day as as an advance party of Welsh horsemen trekked across the desert, one of their number saw the valley below them, fresh and green. "Dyma gwm hyfryd," cried one. And Cwm Hyfryd (Pleasant Valley) it has been since. Two years later wagonloads of families mare the great trek westwards; the towns of Trevelin and Esquel were founded and the success of the Welsh gentle colonisation, without a single battle, had been assured. It was a staggering achievement.

Few Welshmen would not wish to visit this South American Wales and Kyffin was not one of them. He felt the story of the expatriates ought to be recorded in pictures. His enthusiasm persuaded the trustees of the Winston Churchill Memorial Trust to finance this ambition. Kyffin planned to spend four months in the Welsh province of Chubut making a record in pictures. Ideally he would have spent the time capturing on canvas the people, the plants, the flowers, birds, animals and landscape. He realised there was not time for this and decided to let the subject dictate and to record it as simply and directly as possible

It was still a monumental undertaking. Oils were out of the question. The sheer weight of the paints would be prohibitive in view of the huge areas he planned to cover. So he took water colours, designers' colours, coloured inks, pads of paper and a small forest of pencils. On October 16th 1968 he set sail for South America. From Buenos Aires he flew down to Trelew the capitol of Welsh Patagonia.

His arrival in the narrow valley of Chubut was a culture shock. The sense of isolation and the immensity of the place was terrifying. Nothing had prepared him for this narrow valley sunk below cliffs that called to mind Caerphilly cheese, marking the edge of hundreds of miles of desert. The wind blew continually, raising dust storms and battering the small oases of willow, poplars and tamarisk which the early settlers had planted for protection round their farms. But the welcome from their descendants, who through close intermarriage had evolved into a gentle people, was warm. He found a people so gentle that they could not bear to kill the birds that devoured their crops. An artist could not have wished for more. The birds had in consequence become tame and took no notice when Kyffin went to draw them.

At first he used coloured inks but found them too unsubtle and coarse, so he turned to drawing with a Black Prince pencil, using colour as notes. The more he worked the more confident he became. Soon he was using gouache freely to record the wind blasting through the poplars and willows.

The predominant colour was yellow. The desert, the birds, the cactus and spring flowers. He rejoiced in the flamboyant yellow breast of a shrike like bird, a bente-veo; the uracca, a yellow and green jay shrieked amongst orchards and plantations of peach whilst a large professorial bird, the bandurria, uttered a monosyllabic honk. In the cliffs parrots nested in their thousands. Handsome birds with blue green backs and yellow breasts, red splashed. They swept down on the farms in screeching raids but the farmers let them be. Indeed Kyffin's host, Henry Roberts brought one in which had eaten too much to fly. Whereas his tough Welsh forebears would have knocked it on the heads without a second thought. Roberts looked after it until it was fit to fly back to its clifftop nest. Kyffin was delighted, not only at the humanitarian gesture but at the opportunity it gave him to draw it in water colour, catching the subtle relationship between green and blue and yellow. Drawing so much meant he had many failures but it became such a natural thing to do that he felt strange when he did not have pencil or fine brush in his hand. He developed there a love of drawing that stayed with him all his life.

The first settlers had landed at Madryn and Kyffin drew the caves where they had huddled for comfort from the bitter Antarctic gales. he drew irrigation ditches with water wheels on their banks, extracting water with cans fastened to the paddles. He noticed how the water was dropped into a tank and carried away by pipe.

Gradually the despair that had engulfed him fell away as he recorded lingering sunsets that moved and twisted blood red and orange in the sky. After a month in Dyffryn Camwy, on the east coast, he began to feel a great love for the place. What had been daunting had become beautiful; a beauty of contrast with cliffs brooding over all. But he ad to move on to the other part of the colony, Cwm Hyfryd, in the Andean foothills four hundred miles to the west. A mountain man Kyffin looked forward to this as the apogee of the trip. But as he climbed aboard an old Mercedes bus at 5.15 one morning to cross the desert, he was told by his new friends who gathered to see him off at Gaiman that he would return.

Dawn came an hour after the rattling bus had left Gaiman. A desert dawn, a cracking,vivid orange that swept across the sky but soon the dirt road dived towards the Chubut River and the strange rocks that bordered it. His destination, Las Plumas, an untidy group of houses, was bathed in sunlight when they reached it. Chestnut colour and cream-bellied guanaco, the Patagonian llamas, more elegant than the coarse Peruvian breed moved gracefully among coarse shrubs. By now Kyffin was drawing frantically, making hundreds of small notes in a diary in the hope that when he reached Esquel and the Andes he could turn them into gouaches. They were almost diaries in themselves littered with 'pink', 'too steep', 'flatter' and 'stratified'.

He ventured beyond the great cliffs of Los Altares to the Passo de Indios where the desert began and flocks of ostriches grazed and preened themselves before racing away like fully feathered arrows. Those impressions too went down in his diary, fast becoming a disorganised mass of scribbles. Recording, recording he went further into the desert with its strange outcrops of rock –

scribble, scribble – with the sun beating down as it passed over them and ran before. By the time they reached the luscious green valley Nant y Pysgod the sun was descending behind the distant Andes and Kyffin's head was throbbing with pain. Continually drawing under the blazing sun produced an agonising migraine. By the time the bus rattled into Esquel he could hardly see. He was taken in by a kindly Welsh couple. He slept for twelve hours but when he awoke he immediately went back to his 'diaries' as he had come to think of his sketch books.

In a small shed in the couple's garden he produced the series of gouaches which were determine the direction his art took. They were like nothing he had ever drawn before, flat, simple and colourful. Fed and rested, he looked around him at the amazing landscape. The mountains above Esquel were topped in red light and in the distance the Cordilleras reared up, pinnacled and snow capped. He was in the land of the horsemen who arrogantly and superbly rode their strong high stepping horses with one shoulder thrust forward like the Venetian Colleoni statue. Scribble, scribble scribble. They went down in the diaries with drawings of birds completely different from the flocks in Dyffryn Camwy.

To the south lay Cwm Hyfryd and one day Kyffin climbed into a bus owned by a South American called Dennis Jones, and went down a road that resembled a ploughed field until another green valley stretched before him. A great bowl of fine agricultural land under the magnificent snow capped peak of Gorsedd y Cwmyd (throne in the clouds).

In Trevelin in the centre of the valley Kyffin was welcomed by Senora Gwenonwy Berwyn de Jones to her small house, Ty Ni. When he had moved in the Senora introduced him to the family of Indians she had adopted. Out came the diaries and the pencil began to fly. He was especially attracted to a tiny girl Norma who had huge eyes and made a lovely and delightful model.

The new landscape around him was more like Scotland than Wales. Colours were richer and the area vaster. Immensely beautiful, but it never caught at his heart in the way the lower valleys by the sea had. In the evenings the sky was a deep blue black turning the brown land orange. In Dyffryn Camwy the villages had sheltered behind poplars and willows. In the high mountains whirling clouds burst through peaks and sudden cyclones shivered the windows in the houses. It was not water colour land. Gouache was the medium for the rich, rugged valley.

Kyffin was loaned a piebald horse as transport. It seemed a good idea and a convenient way to tour the valley, but he soon discovered drawing from the saddle was difficult and the view from ground level differed in subtle ways from the higher prospect of the saddle.

Yet it was the horse that took him to the greatest triumph of his village. he rode to a farm called Fron Deg where he met a patriarch, a tall, spare 88 year old called Brychan Evans with a distinguished head and the springy bow legs of the horseman. In Evans's parlour Kyffin tried to record his proud head as the patriarch sat looking out of the window at the distant mountains that had been his life. The drawing would not work. Kyffin was incapable of doing the grand old man justice. Part in temper and part depressed he returned to his room at Ty Ni. For hours he wrestled with that wonderful face until at last he produced a water colour portrait that satisfied him. It was not only like Evans, it was the head of all the Patagonian Welshmen who had won a living against terrific odds. Kyffin felt that portrait alone justified his four months of almost continually painting and drawing.

Years later he was to write "My visit to the Welsh in Patagonia was of the utmost value to my art. I was there for a purpose which drove me to draw with an intensity that had never been possible before. To make such a record as I did in Patagonia is a great incentive and it imposes discipline, essential to a writer or a musician but often forgotten by painters."

Patagonia always held a special place in his heart. When in 1991 he published the second volume of biographical notes, *A Wider Sky*, the account of his Patagonian adventure was a high spot. "They didn't know what to make of me. My Welsh was catastrophic and they said I didn't speak Welsh, but for me it was the most exciting and memorable period of my life."

EIGHT

In 1970 when Kyffin was elected a Royal Academician he decided to give up teaching altogether and return to Wales. Four years later, an increasingly popular painter with the art buying public, he came home to Anglesey. He told me: "I could not stay in London. I was becoming psychophrenic in my painting. In Wales I looked at the mountains and felt wonderful. I knew exactly what I wanted to paint. When I got back to London, like most Welshmen I became possessed by a fatal Cymric nostalgia which blotted out what I wanted to say in my pictures."

People who love Anglesey have difficulty in persuading outsiders of its special quality. Mainlanders claim that its main function is as a platform from which to view the beauties of Snowdonia. Those fortunate enough to live there know that at the beguiling heart of its appeal is a sense of ancient place. Anglesey was the last stonghold of the Druids in Europe. The names of its fields – The Field of the Long Battle, the Field of Bitter Lamentation in the parish of Brynsiencyn – recall the Roman invasion; a house called Shoutton an eminence from which tribesmen could see the Strait recalls warnings of the Norsemen.

When RAF Valley was under construction during the early part of the Second World War the runway was made of packed sand. In order to bind it, workmen brought tons of mud from Llyn Cerrig Bach, which in the dark Age of the Princes had been a lake. When a tractor stuck in the mud it was hauled out with a chain which proved to be a Celtic slave chain. Fortunately it was identified. The driver told of finding it in the mud. Excavations discovered a hoard of weapons and chariot harness. It is believed they were thrown in the lake by Druids seeking to placate an ancient war god. Might not the story of Excalibur been a folk memory of that tradition?

Kyffin had never lost touch with the island home of his ancestors. His cousin Betty Mewies knows how important the island
was to him: "Kyffin always said what he thinks. I think the reason
was that he was so secure and the reason for that is Anglesey. He
felt so right there. He was part of it and it gave him a security
which allowed him to say what he liked. Our family tree goes back
to the eleventh century. All on Anglesey."

Wendy Davies recalled that her "great Aunt Cecily Vivian had
the Anglesey Beagles after the war, and Kyffin and I hunted a lot
with them. Great Aunt Cecily played a big part in his life. She was
a really sparky old lady. She was a very positive woman. If he was
in one of his dumps you would here her say 'If you are in the
dumps you can turn round and go home.' She gave him a lot of
support. Although she had this tough exterior she had a great
appreciation of art." But she was certainly tough. On one
occasion she went hunting in Ireland with her husband, Cyril. At
one hunt Cyril came off. Someone came up to Aunt Cecily with
the news. ""As she galloped after the hounds Aunt Cecily called
over her shoulder, 'Send him to the kennels'."

Wendy's grandfather was very scornful of Anglesey families:
"All they do is chase girls, empty bottles and litigate." Kyffin had
a much higher opinion of the island's leading families. There was
just a suggestion of benevolent snob about the way he cherished
them. Certainly he knew their histories and could be wildly indis-
creet. At one dinner table he enlarged on his belief that no leading
Anglesey family was what it seemed:

> There is no family as old as mine in the direct line. The Bulkeleys
> are really Williamses, the Pagets are really Baileys and the Lloyds
> are Jones Parrys. The reason is evident. People changed their
> names to inherit land. Anglesey is an odd place.
>
> In the eighteenth century Anglesey was ruled by its squires.
> They were a benevolent group and on the rise of non-
> conformism the squires made generous gifts of land to the
> chapels. Little did they realise they were building Trojan horses.
> The chapels bred resentment of the squirearchy and by the
> beginning of the nineteenth century power had been transferred
> to the chapels. The squires had nothing left but their pedigrees.
> So they retreated to their houses only communicating with other

land owners and comparing the length of their family trees. They
became the most monumental snobs. They were known as the
toffee noses of North Wales. The families are riven with feuds.
Before there were bridges over the Strait, feuding and cohabiting
were all they did.

I remember a terrible feud about the sacking of a huntsman of
the Anglesey Hounds. My great uncle Tom Rice Roberts was
master and he appointed a man called Davies as huntsman. He
was always drunk. Everyone drank; there was nothing else to do.
The mastership was taken over by Evelyn Meyrick who sacked
Davies. Anglesey was riven.

There was a GP in Llangefni, Dr Llywelyn Jones. He was
terribly keen on getting in with the Anglesey gentry so he went
out hunting beautifully turned out. Top hat, green coat and a nice
horse. Fine figure of a man and very popular with the wives of
members. His progeny under other names are in the island now.
There are some people on the island who are related to me but
they do not know it and would be horrified if they did. Hanky
panky was known in Anglesey as having a gallop

Kyffin's knowledge of Anglesey pedigrees was encyclopedic:

A man called Williams left the Vaynol estate across the Straits
from us to George II. The King didn't want it so he gave it in
turn to a minor court functionary called Smith. He added
Assheton to his name. What the King did not know was that the
land included much of Snowdonia and the quarries were to bring
the Assheton Smiths an enormous fortune. An Assheton Smith
heiress married a Robin Duff who became Duff Assheton Smith.
His son Michael Duff married the Marquess of Anglesey's elder
sister Caroline, one of the great beauties of the day. His sister
married a Lord Glenconner who was a Tennant. When Michael
Duff died the money went to the Tennants.

Michael Duff and Caroline had an adopted child Charlie but
he did not inherit. Caroline was the painter Rex Whistler's great
love and a great friend of Tallulah Bankhead. She would have
married Rex but he was killed in the war when he got out of his
tank under heavy fire to free it from wire.

The Queen Mother was a frequent visitor to Vaynol and Tony
Armstrong-Jones was Michael Duff's godson. I knew his great
aunt. His uncle, a man called Howden Armstrong-Jones lived in
Eisteddfa, a house near ours on the Lleyn near Criccieth. He
wore loud checks and put on a Welsh accent. My father hated
him but his sister Jinnie Armstrong Jones was lovely. She called
me her little platinum. Armstrong Jones was always pestering

Lloyd George for a knighthood, In the end he got one by mistake. It should have gone to another Armstrong Jones from Liverpool.

They were offspring of a parson who had no money. No-one knew how they became rich until I looked into the pedigrees and found there was a brother who was the Director of the Indian Mint.

Perhaps the two people Kyffin most dearly loved were the Marquess and Marchioness of Anglesey. He dedicated *A Wider Sky* to the Marchioness, and told in it how they found him the home on their estate, a converted inn at Pwllfanogl where he lived until his death. He described it to a friend:

> I live and work on the edge of an old harbour. The waters of the Menai Strait wash almost to my front door and the River Braint flows through the woods behind the house, under a bridge and through the harbour to the Strait a hundred yards from my front door.
>
> There could be no better place for an artist to live, for across the Strait I can see the mountains, the Carneddau, Elidir Fawr, Snowdon and the hills that edge down to Pen Lleyn. The great bow of the Strait bends westwards to Caernarfon and the Open Sea. To the East it winds through the Swellie Rocks, under the bridges to the Great Orme at Llandudno. Fishermen launch their boats at the front of my house and the Bangor trawlers make for Porth Penrhyn with accompanying seagulls crowding in their wake. On summer evenings terns dive for fish.
>
> On the longest day of the year the sun rises over the island above the spire of Llanfairpwllgwyngyll church and for six months I watch it rising until on December 22 it appears over the Western slopes of Elidir. Throughout the year it creates a footpath of light across the water to my house.
>
> I make colour notes and later try to turn them into paintings in my studio in the garden. But to me, painting the sea is a battle like the one the sea fights with the land. I aim to keep the picture fluid and the paint rich and sensuous. But it is so difficult to get the light to rest on the sea in the right perspective and so easy to lose it by some ill-judged movement of the brush.

In *A Wider Sky* Kyffin told of a small boy who visited him at Pwllfanogl

As we stood at the waters edge with gentle waves breaking at our feet the little boy looked up at me.

"What will happen to you here when you die?" he asked with a look of concern on his face. I knew I had to answer with a confidence I did not possess.

"Oh it will be wonderful," I said. "I shall slip into the sea and be swept away by the water and I shall be carried under the bridges and away to Penmon and the open sea. Oh yes it will be rather wonderful...."

His circle of friends did not only embrace the leading families. He loved the country people and drew and painted them endlessly. In the views of many, those portraits and prints were amongst the greatest of his works and the ones that will live the longest. No artist ever got nearer to the hearts of people who would never dream of setting foot in an art gallery. He took them as his subjects. Children who sat for him got half a crown, a cup of tea and a slice of his mother's delicious swiss roll. They also, like his friends, were rewarded with a lifetime's devotion.

One of them, Gwilym Islwyn Owen, sat for the picture which won Kyffin the Slade Portrait Award. Years later in 1989 they met again when Owen was working as a car park attendant in Criccieth. He recalled: "Some weeks later a lady drove up with a parcel for me. It was the painting and it came with a note from Kyffin remembering when it was painted. I will treasure it all my life."

Yet Kyffin could be critical. Shortly after he moved to Pwllfanogl, and before care for the environment became a fashionable issue, he told Arthur Williams, the *Daily Post* columnist, of his worries that the Menai Strait was becoming polluted: "Welsh people are apathetic about their surroundings. Basically it is the English people who are most concerned by the ruination of the landscape. The Welsh are terribly concerned about the language but they don't use their eyes. I find this very extraordinary. If the Welsh Language Society put the same energy into the conservation of the Welsh landscape that they do into the conservation of the language it would be a great benefit to the nation."

The portraits he painted with a palette knife. In his early days he sacrificed accuracy of tone by using a dark line to draw into the thick paint to define each area one from another. But as his confidence grew, he dispensed with the line and painted only tonally and always with a knife. He used few colours because he believed that extra colour complicated the portrait. and the fewer the colours the more accurate the tone must be. His best results were achieved, he thought, with only black, white, cadmium red and yellow ochre.

His most difficult subjects were girls and young women and he reckoned it took him twenty years to learn how to do them. He usually painted old people, farmers, labourers, people in homes for the blind and the old. The blind fascinated him. He wondered at their peaceful resignation, their wet lips always moving and the eternity of space in their dead eyes. He always painted against a flat bright background and when the painting was dry he would take it back to the home of the subject so that he could pass his fingers over the ridge of paint, feeling his ears, his eyes and his hair.

He described painting a Mrs Stanley of Beaumaris in a huge green armchair dressed in an ultramarine frock. She was ninety-two years old, her tiny head covered in lace like hair, her face soft and pink and her long hands moving continually. "As I painted she hummed strange hymn tunes. Occasionally she would break off to utter disconcerting remarks about God's determination to take me as he had taken the rest of her friends. 'You know not the day nor the hour' she warned me. Then she fell asleep and I finished the painting to the sound of her snores, mixed with the cry of the seagulls and the cars in the street below."

Other sittings were less tranquil. An Anglesey farmer sat on an oak settle. The flickering flames from the kitchen fire danced on his cheeks making it difficult to find the right tone and colour. At last Kyffin gave up and the farmer came over to see what he had done. "Well, well, well," he said in his slow Anglesey voice. "Everything is so wrong. My motor is broke down, my tractor's big end has gone, my milking machine won't work, and now you can't paint my face." Anglesey farmers have mixed views about artists.

At Benllech on Anglesey Kyffin's car became stuck in wet sand and a farmer used a chain and a Fergy tractor to haul him out. In gratitude, Kyffin, who had no money, tore the painting he had just completed off his sketching block and gave it to the farmer. Then watched in horror as the farmer folded the painting into quarters and stuffed in his overall pocket.

When he decided to live in Pwllfanogl he went to see an old lady, Maggie Williams Penymynydd, who used to help his mother in the house. She was a huge, raw boned woman, humorous and very earthy. She told him if was going there he would have to find a woman. Kyffin jibbed: "What if we don't get on?" She replied. "If you don't get on? Duw, it's a grand place to drown the bugger."

When he came home after being discharged from the army he was sent to an old family nurse, Sarah Richards. One day she said she had a treat for him. "I am going to take you to Bonnw where my brother Bob lives. I will introduce you to his house-keeper Miss Hughes. She has three daughters and neither one of them is sisters."

Kyffin's kingdom is intensely partisan. Painting in Cwm Bychan he got out of his car to feel a presence behind him. He turned to see a short, stocky aboriginal Welshwoman who rapped out in Welsh "ten pence!" He told her he was Welsh. "Where do you come from?" she asked. "Ynys Mon" he told her. "That will be twenty pence," she replied.

Kyffin's cultural contribution to that kingdom has been immense and is widely recognised. Less well known is the work he did silently for charity. Dr Jim Davies and his wife Nesta worked tirelessly for charities in North Wales and between them raised millions of pounds. They said people did not realise how much Kyffin had given in the way of pictures and prints. Nesta told me: "We never hear about the pictures and prints he gave to charities. I know he was very kind to me when I was working with muscular dystrophy but he is generous to so many causes you cannot list them. He paints austere mountains and is like a rock himself. He is a deep as the sea but he is full of humour."

Dr Jim was one of Wales's doughtiest fighters. During the war he was a special services wireless operator who flew on bomber raids in a plane which went in before the bombers to jam the German equipment. It was incredibly dangerous. Of the seven sergeant who joined his squadron two were killed and he was was shot down on his second mission. For six months he lived with the Dutch resistance until a double agent betrayed him to the Gestapo. He was sent to a series of POW camps before being force-marched hundreds of miles from Stalag Luft 7 from Poland to Berlin. After the war he was appointed Principal of Bangor Normal College. When senior civil servants in the Ministry of Education decided to close it, Dr Jim organised the campaign to keep it open and led an all parliamentary deputation to the Secretary of State for Education, Fred Mullay. He said he would give them five minutes but they were with him for two hours. Subsequently he decided to reverse the decision to close. It was the only time he rejected the advice of his top civil servants who wanted to close it as part of a policy of rationalisation. Instead it lives on as part of the University of Wales. How did Dr Jim persuade the Minister? "Lord Cledwyn tipped me off the Fred Mullay had also been a prisoner of war and advised me to mention my POW days. So talking about the Butler 1944 education act, I said at that time we were both guests of the fuhrer." It worked.

Dr Jim recalled the fund he ran to raise funds for a scanner at Ysbyty Gwynedd: "We were determined the new building would be friendly, artistic and exciting. So you may imagine how delighted we were when Kyffin gave us prints for every wall and promised to do the same for a new haematology and cancer unit. He kept his promise.

Dr Jim explained the hurdle painters have to leap for acceptance in Wales:

> Painting and the visual arts are not part of the Welsh cultural background. We were brought up on literature and music, the Eisteddfod culture. Sometimes we do not take painting seriously enough. When I spoke at the Cambrian Academy Summer Exhibition in 1998, I supported Kyffin's view that it was a disgrace that in the magnificent National Art Gallery and Museum in Cardiff there was not a single room devoted to Welsh art. The first curator had said such a room would diminish our European contribution. Rubbish, said Kyffin, and I agreed with him. Cardiff is a significant capital and I am delighted that at last Kyffin was listened to and our national art has a fitting home there.

There were no patrons here. In Europe you had the church, in England powerful aristocrats. In Wales you only had the things that were free. The voice and the word. And the non-conformist tradition took no account of the visual arts. The economy in Wales was based on pastoral farming, which meant there was no money for painting and sculpture. Wales had to express itself in the cheapest way possible By word and song.

Kyffin fought ceaselessly for a place in the Welsh sun for its painters. He was twice President of the Royal Cambrian Academy of Welsh Art, persuading some of the finest artists in Wales to exhibit at its superb modern gallery in Conwy. Vicky MacDonald, the Director remembered

> He was a superb chairman and because of his stature commanded respect all over the art world. His first stint as president ended acrimoniously in 1976 when our headquarters was in an Elizabethan mansion in the town, Plas Mawr. It was owned by Lord Mostyn, who told us that the house was in very bad condition and needed half a million pounds spending on it.
> He agreed the Cambrian had a 99 year lease and could not be moved but urged us to move. At Kyffin's suggestion, he offered us a purpose built gallery, what is now the Mostyn, a purpose-built gallery in Llandudno at a very reasonable rent. However the members did not want to move and Kyffin resigned in despair.

Over the years standards fell at the Cambrian until it became little more than a sketching club. When, after a brilliantly success-ful fund raising campaign organised by a subsequent President Jack Shore and his committee the Academy was able to move into a new purpose built gallery, Kyffin agreed to come back as president. Said Vicky:

> He immediately took the responsibility for raising the standards and included Article 15 in the charter by which artists of quality could be invited to become members without having to pass scrutiny by the Academy members. He was the ideal president. He was always ready to help in any way he could. Rarely missed a meeting unless he was ill and bubbled with new ideas. He knew everyone in the art world and certainly knew how the art world works.

Outside art, it was a casual meeting on a railway station which launched Kyffin on a new career as an author. Anna Haycraft was waiting on a platform at Euston Station for a train home to Penmaenmawr. She had been working at Cheshire Homes but was disillusioned with Captain Cheshire, whose ideas on hygiene she found bizarre. She decided to leave and go into a convent. Kyffin recalled seeing this very attractive girl and introducing himself. "We talked all the way to Penmaenmawr where her mother lived. She said she was going into a convent and I thought what a terrible waste. She did go into the convent but she slipped a disc, had to go to hospital and never went back. She married the publisher Colin Haycraft and they had seven children. I fell in love with her the first time we met."

Anna who became a best-selling novelist as Alice Thomas Ellis remember their 'Brief Encounter':

> It was forty years ago and I was an art student. There was this man and we got into conversation. I thought he was absolutely fascinating. I didn't see him for a few years, then it was by chance. Freddy Uhlman was a mutual friend, Colin and I went to his house and there was this delightful person I had met by chance. I had never forgotten him but I believed I would never see again. We have been friends ever since. I didn't know he was in love with me. I love Kyffin, I always have.
>
> Kyffin is very important in my life because he is one of the very few good people that I know and he is funny with it. He is the best company you could ever have. He is witty and wise and funny. I thought he was wary of marriage because of the epilepsy. In any case, I loved him too much to marry him. I think he was almost too good to marry. I don't know any woman who could have matched up to him. He was so dedicated to his art I think any woman would have felt she took second place to that. I recognised in Kyffin a quality so unusual I do not think it has a name. Purity, perhaps. People you marry you tend to fight with and I could not imagine ever fighting with him.
>
> I cannot imagine Kyffin married. His attraction for women? Can't speak for other women. I just found him incredibly lovable. Other men are attractive physically. He is not only lovable but intensely likable. You never felt threatened by him. He is a very difficult man to encapsulate. My children absolutely doted on him. They called him Uncle Kyffin. He was what I expect an uncle to be and a gentleman too if it comes to that.
>
> As an artist I think he was supreme. Wales is grey and green,

black and white and I think he latched on to that. I don't think
water colours work here and I am sure he is the only painter who
has got Wales as it is.

I have wondered whether the epilepsy had anything to do with
his talent. Interesting how he could stand in a howling gale and
not feel cold at all until he stopped painting.

It was a phenomenon that puzzled Kyffin too. He said: "It is
very odd. I can stand in the snow for hours with the temperature
below freezing point and yet my hands remain warm until I stop
painting. My left hand, which holds the palette, even though
motionless in the frosty air, remains comfortably warm. Only
when I pack up do I feel cold. I imagine that unconsciously I
practise yoga."

Anna has another explanation. "Painting was for Kyffin what
religion is to me. He creates the world that is and adds something
to it. Incidentally, he is wrong about one thing. He said I left the
convent, I did not. The convent slung me out because of the
slipped disc. If you are a postulant and you cannot work you are
no good. I am going back when I get the chance."

It was Anna's husband, Colin, who published in 1973 Kyffin's
first book *Across the Straits*, which he dedicated to her. The book,
a minor classic, caused a storm among the *uchelwyr* of Gwynedd
who considered that in what has become a minor country classic
he told too many of their secrets. Lord Crickhowell revealed that
after the success of *Across the Straits* Kyffin wrote a sequel by
hand and sent it – the only copy – to Duckworth's:

> He wrote it not all that much after *Across the Straits*. His
> publisher insisted it was sent off to a reader despite the success
> of the first book. Unfortunately the reader who was a consider-
> able pornographer got word he might be raided by the police. So
> he burned all the pornographic books. Alas, he included, not I
> think on grounds of pornography, the only text of *A Wider Sky*
> which was as I say hand written. Poor Kyffin was deeply upset
> and it took him a long time before he could bring himself to write
> it again. Not surprisingly it is not as vigorous as *Across the Straits*.

NINE

By 1969 Kyffin had already held thirty one-man exhibitions, but the golden years began in 1970 when he was elected Associate of the Royal Academy. From then until his death honours gathered like swallows on a wire. In 1974 he became a full Royal Academician, in 1978, an Honourary MA of the University of Wales, in 1983 he received an OBE, in 1987 he was appointed a Deputy Lieutenant of Gwynedd, in 1989 he was appointed a Deputy Fellow of the University of Wales, Swansea, in 1991 an Honourary Fellow of the University of Wales, Bangor, and in the same year won the Medal of the Honourable Society of Cymrodorion. In 1992 it was the turn of the University College of Wales, Aberystwyth, to make him an Honorary Fellow. In the same year he became President of the Royal Cambrian Academy for the second time, member of the arts advisory Committee of National Museum of Wales, member of the Court of Governors of the National Library of Wales and to mark its centenary in 1993 the University of Wales made him an Honorary Doctor of Letters in company with the Aga Khan and Mary Robinson, the President of Ireland. The degrees were presented by the Prince of Wales, and in Kyffin's case recognised his six books: *Across the Straits, A Wider Sky, Portraits, Land and Sea,* a Gregynog limited edition of his *Mabinogion* illustrations and a book of cartoons, *Boyo Ballads.* He has also illustrated books for others, including a *Welsh Anthology* by Alice Thomas Ellis, *The Astonishing Infantry; the History of the Royal Welsh Fusiliers* by Michael Glover, *Patagonia Revisited* by Bruce Chatwin and Paul Theroux, and *Two Old Men* by Kate Roberts.

By 1970 he had put on four exhibitions at Colnahgi's, London, six at the Leicester Galleries, London, one at the Glynn Vivian Art

Gallery in Swansea, another at the Howard Roberts Gallery in Cardiff. and five at the Tegfryn Gallery in Menai Bridge. After 1975 he had bi-annual exhibitions at the Thackeray Gallery in London and the Albany Gallery, Cardiff. He was issuing limited editions of greatly sought after prints, painting two pictures a week and living a very full social life until his final illness.

His greatest moment came with the New Year Honours in 1999 when he was given a knighthood in recognition of his services to the visual arts. He was delighted. He felt that his wars with the establishment had been vindicated by the establishment itself. He was very happy, too, that the first letter of congratulations came from the Prince of Wales. He held the Prince in high esteem and the feeling was obviously reciprocated.

His army of friends were delighted, though some were apprehensive that he might not turn up for the Investiture. They recalled his eightieth birthday celebrations when the various organisations to which he contributed so much sought to honour him with presentations. Among them, Wales Tourist Board arranged a reception at the Royal Academy with a show of his Patagonian paintings to which the Argentinian ambassador was invited. Kyffin pleaded illness and did not attend. Other presentations shared the same fate. He made a brief appearance at an Arts Fund luncheon, but only because it was at Plas Newydd, the home of his great friends the Marquess and Marchioness of Anglesey, and then only for a few minutes at the end of the lunch.

True, he had hired a morning coat to attend his OBE investiture. But even the there was a contretemps. Walking across to the Palace he felt a tabbing pain in his foot. When he examined the shoe he found there was a hole in it. Looking round for something to cover it, all he could find was an empty cheese flavoured crisp packet. Folding it, he slipped it into the shoe. It was comfortable enough but as he waited for his turn to be invested his nostrils were assailed by the smell of cheese. The warmth of the room had released the aroma from the packet. Urgently Kyffin asked a passing courtier if he had some spare paper. The courtier obliged, then watched with a amazement as Kyffin took off his shoe, removed the crisp packet and replaced it with the paper. "Thank you. That is much better," he told the courtier.

In 1998 the Prince of Wales had invited him to Highgate to see his water colours. Clearly too shy to discuss them, he did not meet Kyffin after he had seen them. The Prince need not have worried. Kyffin was very impressed. "Some were very good indeed."

There were increasing signs that the Establishment was taking him to its bosom. A fortnight after the knighthood the Welsh Secretary Alun Michael 'dropped in' on Kyffin at Pwllfanogl. He told a reporter who just happened to be there what a huge fan of Kyffin's he was, and how he had bought a treasured copy of Kyffin's *The Land and the Sea*. He continued, "I think most people would be jealous of my having the opportunity to meet Kyffin. "You don't often have the chance to say thank you to somebody who has given so much pleasure to me and to countless other people. I think he reflects the sort of confidence and pride we need in things that are Welsh. I was delighted to hear of his knighthood. It reflected something which many people throughout Wales wanted to say. His paintings have captured something that is very important combining art with the mood of the countryside, the mountains, the weather and the sea."

Mr Michael confided that one of Kyffin's lino cuts hung on the wall of his House of Commons' office and there are two of his paintings graced the walls of the Welsh office. It was a charming tribute but cynical observers noted Mr Michael was in the middle of an election battle with Rhodri Morgan for the Leadership of the Welsh Assembly.

Not all the Royal Family were Kyffin fans. A large and very fine painting he had presented to the Princess Royal mysteriously surfaced some years later at an Anglesey auction house. For his part, Kyffin pretended not to be impressed with the knighthood. As with everything that happened to him, he turned it into an anecdote to amuse his friends. "When Downing Street rang to ask me if I would accept one I thought they were joking. Odd business. When the letter came it had two boxes and you had to tick a 'yes' box if you wanted a knighthood and a 'no' box if you did not."

His friend Lord Crickhowell is a perceptive critic of Kyffin's work:

There was a period when his painting was very dark. We always used to say Kyffin "Can't you brighten up?" But he could not. Then suddenly, as he got older, he seemed to break out of this dark period and started painting seascapes with great flaring suns, scarlets and yellows was. Its really quite a recent development. At his '98 Albany exhibition there were some tremendous snowscapes. Painting of a kind that twenty years ago you would never have seen them.

His cartoons are another recent development. He gave me a very amusing cartoon about my trouble with the plan for a Cardiff Opera House. It shows an opera singer and a rugby player. On another occasion he was helping my daughter Olivia to paint and there was paint all over the kitchen. My wife told them off and that produced another cartoon.

He remained very much the 'Painter of Gwynedd', as he was described at the beginning of his career. It is interesting that though he often stayed with us in the Black Mountains he could not paint there. He was most at home in North Wales. He could paint in Pembroke because of the sea. But he seemed not to be able to catch the gentle softness of the Black Mountains; perhaps even the light. Light was very important to him. I always thought it had something to do with his epilepsy. Clearly it affected the way he painted. Epileptics are profoundly affected by light. My wife who had a mild epileptic condition hates sitting under strobe lamps. They have an immediate effect on her.

Whatever the reason he didn't paint here, alas. It is that tremendous sense of drama and light and dark of North Wales which he didn't find in Breconshire. I have one drawing. It's about the only one he has ever done in all the years he stayed here, or before that at my father's cottage across the bridge

Crickhowell's father, Ralph Edwards, discussing Kyffin's drawings in 1964, drew attention to Kyffin's devotion to his own land:

Kyffin Williams is amongst the most gifted contemporary painters for whom nature has continued to suffice. He is a Welsh artist in the romantic tradition (as were J.D. Innes and Augustus John) and his art is deeply imbued with the Celtic spirit; which is recognisable in the work of his elder contemporaries – in the visionary world of David Jones and in Ceri Richards's colour and rhythms.

He has a deep feeling for a type of scenery with which he has been familiar since childhood and an intuitive understanding of its essential characteristics, which an alien can scarcely obtain.

His drawings are those of a painter. Many are in fact studies for paintings, all done on the spot. His oils and his drawings are unmistakably by the same hand. In the drawings, broad washes are often put on with a full brush and the thick contour lines are sharply defined.

When colour is used at all in his preparatory studies it is used sparingly in a scale of muted hues; volumes, forms, atmosphere and distances are rendered largely by strong contrasts of tone, the white of the paper being often foiled against black. Thus resonant effects of light and dark are obtained with plastic illusion, ink wash being the medium most often employed. But this is no facile formula or convention; the drawings are interpretative, expressing a highly personal vision – the spirit in preference to the physical facts. It is not gentle nor elegiac nor does it breathe the *douce melancholie de la campagne*; the landscape of the artist's predilection is far from sweet: much of it is melancholy, sombre or austere...

...his vigorous, expressive style, which has no close parallel and is identifiable at a glance, is admirably adapted to record his subjective impressions of nature.

Professor David Carpanini RA has the Chair of Fine Art at the University of Wolverhampton and is President of the Royal Society of Painters and Printmakers. He met Kyffin when they were both elected to the Academy in 1974. He says quite simply:

To call Kyffin a friend has been an honour and a privilege and I am one of many who has been inspired by his enormous knowledge of art, his generosity of spirit and his artistic integrity.

I was always impressed by the his extraordinary generosity to young artists once he sensed they were making an effort to work towards their vision. He must have been a charismatic teacher at Highgate. Although he always made light of his time there, I remember when we had a house at Llanberis he brought round a portfolio of the boys' work. My wife Janet and I were struck by the way he knew exactly what had happened to all of them. Of course he had distinguished pupils like Patrick Proctor and Anthony Green but there were others who did not go into the world of art. What was impressive about the portfolio was that there was no evidence of a house style. No one had tried to imitate Kyffin. They were trying to follow their own visions. That is the mark of a good teacher.

I find it extraordinary that he did not get wide recognition from the UK establishment and from those self-appointed arbiters of taste with their prejudices and fashions who could not see in him what he truly was, a major contemporary painter. He consistently followed a strong personal vision with total truth and I think that is what the public recognise, perhaps without knowing it, and why they appreciate him so much.

He never found painting or drawing easy. But he loved his subject and struggled to find a consistent quality of 'newness'. He was never a repeatist artist. There was a variety in the way he handled his subject which was mesmeric. His paintings work on two levels. They have a strong narrative and at the same time an aesthetic appeal. Great art must work on those levels and that is the reason I believe his work will live long after most of his more fashionable contemporaries are forgotten.

It is a measure of his painting that you do not have to look for clever words to respond to it. The way he applies paint to a canvas could be deterrent but it is not. There is an abstract quality which is very engaging. He articulates his vision so precisely and his method of doing so is at one with his spiritual dimension. The public sense that his pictures are right.. Here is honesty and truth. They have all stood on a headland and felt the seas spray in their face. Here it is on canvas.

Anyone who goes to art with an open mind and heart is rewarded. It is only the person who brings their baggage of prejudice who cannot see its quality.

It was difficult to get Kyffin to talk of his methods, though much was written about him and he was filmed many times. At the time Edwards was writing (see page 121, above) Kyffin spoke in an interview about his style. Thirty years later he agreed it had altered little.

First I lay in the outlines of my subject with a brush. Then also with a brush I cover the whole area with a tone darker than my final painting. I do this because I can let the dark through here and there as I want to give points of vitality and strength to the picture. I use very little white at this stage to avoid chalkiness.

The palette I use in the studio is flake white, ivory black, Windsor yellow, yellow ochre, burnt umber, cobalt blue and cobalt green. Outdoors I add vermillion and French ultramarine. You must have vermillion for bracken. I use flake white in preference to titanium or zinc white because they have no weight for my knife.

When I paint mountains I know what is on the other side. For eighteen months at the Slade I floundered hopelessly. All the other students seemed so brilliant. Their line drawing was

uncanny and their general air of artistic awareness was frighten-
ing. One day Professor Schwabe was giving me a lesson in line
drawing. He advised me to paint but at first I could find impulse
nor enthusiasm to pull me along and make up from my lack of
facility.

And then one day in the Ashmolean I saw a reproduction of
Pierro della Francesca's 'Resurrection.' I realised then how much
really did come from things, from people, from the hills and
mountains; from rivers and waterfalls and the sea and how much
I wanted to paint them.

So I started to paint seriously. I worked fast since I was so
desperate to see my pictures finished and alive in front of me.
The great library of my boyhood experiences came back to me
as if I had filed them away for this purpose. I was twenty-four
and had been an art student for 18 months. I was beginning to
find myself and all the energy that had made me pursue unfortunate foxes, and made me dream of cavalry charges, winning
the Grand National or scoring a winning try for Wales was put
into painting the things I began to realise I loved dearly.

From that moment there was no search for technique. My
intense interest was to put down what I saw; what was in my
mind dictated how it was done. I found myself painting in a
manner that surprised me and one in which I had never seen a
picture painted before. They may have been poor things but at
least they were my own. I began to realise how lucky I was to
have been brought up in the countryside. The scudding light on
a hillside suddenly became more exciting, more electric. The
heavy cloud over Snowdon more moving. I found myself walking
miles over the mountains, making hundreds of drawings, carrying paints and canvases up onto windy ridges and down the
screes, seeking out the places I had known so well in the past.

Shortly before his death, Kyffin looked back over the years
between that eager young man and the present, when he was
widely acknowledged as Wales's greatest living painter.

People assume that painting is a pleasure. I don't enjoy painting,
there is the pressure and the duty. You cannot afford to luxuriate.
You have to put it on canvas. And there are seasons like spring
and autumn when painting is very difficult indeed. In spring you
get the mountains still dressed for winter. Cold, blue grey.
Against them you get the lemon of a sycamore in the valleys. I
only once managed to paint that well. In a picture called 'Lleder
Valley in Spring'.

It bothered me until I realised that none of the great artists had ever painted spring or autumn successfully. Turner did vaguely but Constable didn't. It never works over grass because green and brown just don't go together and green is just so difficult. I now mute a rich green and in some ways that is a lie. But it is the only way colours work.

It was important to Kyffin to relate to the people, which is why his paintings cost so little in comparison to the price lesser painters charge. He explained:

In the past ministers, miners and farmers could not buy paintings. Now thanks to improved education their sons entered the professions and have a larger disposable income but its still not too large. I coming from the same roots as they do painted the places they wanted to be reminded of.

I am the first Welsh painter who has been able to live and work in Wales. I may also be the first artist to get through to the Welsh public but I have never appealed to the art establishment. Being the only Welsh born RA was unfortunate because they resented it. There is something in the Welsh character that is displeased by success in England. Welsh people were often nominated but they attracted very few votes. I am glad the Welsh people like my work and call me Kyffin.

My development has been very gradual because I never considered myself a serious painter until the Sixties when a particularly offensive landlady threw me out on a trumped up charge of offending her daily. I had to find alternative accommodation I went round studios and found they were all occupied by old women with cats. I got so angry hat I realised I had got hooked on painting. Before that I thought I was painting for the good of my health. I never kept a record of the paintings I sold. I did not have any ambition to be a proper painter. I wanted to teach in an art school but no art school would have me because it was the time when they were jettisoning the idea of drawing. However incapable I might have been at the Slade, if you are obsessed, as I luckily have been, obsession can create talent. I am not a natural draughtsman.but I was so obsessed with recording Wales and its people it forced me to learn how to draw. I have never wanted to change my style, just to paint better and there was a lot of room.

I started selling well when I moved my exhibitions from Bond Street to Kensington in 1974. I have had twelve exhibitions in Kensington, one every other year and on each occasion. I have sold better. Partly because my pictures are cheap. Most artists charge too much and then complain that they don't sell. If they worked harder and sold for less they would sell more. But artists think they are great and have to put whacking great prices on their work.

I do not know why people like my work. I don't particularly. There are none in my house. I couldn't bear to have them in the house.

I had wonderful preparation for the life of an artist. The worst thing is to be eulogised when you are young. With me it has been a gradual climb and just right. I have never actually considered I am a success. If I did it would be the end. If any artist ever thinks he has arrived he has had it. I have had a very odd life. Very strange. I tried to do anything but paint. It was a very gradual process. I suppose I didn't mind getting kicked. I began to relish it. Terrible insults. I have always been ignored or insulted but it has been water off a duck's back

People won't take to me because I use a palette knife. It's alright to cut a sheep in half but a palette knife is out. You can use your nose or a tooth brush, but never a palette knife but I have never bothered about rules. I use a palette knife because I like the sheer thickness of paint, the sensuality of it. I think I spend most of my money on paint.

Now I find that though my palette hasn't great altered I am using a lot of slake white, which in oil painting is the equivalent of water. I am not a colourist. A colourist is like a juggler. He throws ten different colours in the air. I can only juggle with three. I learned to paint with a fairly restricted palette and there is a sort of rhetoric in my work which is best translated into fewer colours.

For me painting has always been a matter of instinct. In your subconscious you know what you are doing. But the more it comes from the head, the less likely you are to be able to communicate it. I love certain things and I am able to communicate them. Contemporary art tends to be pretentious and communicates itself to pretentious people.

I don't want to have exhibitions now, I have had so many. I don't want to sell pictures. I hate continually painting pictures which go out of my studio straight away. I want to look at them. My gallery in London want a Millennium exhibition but I don't. I want to send my best work to the RA. I don't think the RA will last. They are letting in so many people who cannot draw. When drawing comes back they won't know how to teach it. They will be left high and dry. Drawing will come back. People are bound to love the world around them and the only way you can show appreciation is by putting it down. If you are not equipped to put it down there is nothing else to do but sheep in formaldehyde.

Kyffin was always been dismissive of his own work. When he was fifty-eight he told a critic, "At my age artists don't improve. All I hope is that I don't get any worse."

The most scholarly study of Kyffin work has been written by the distinguished scholar Professor Alistair Crawford, the founder and former head of the School of Art at the University of Wales, Aberystwyth, himself a successful artist, photographer and print maker his work in private collections all over the world. He was a student at Glasgow School of Art when he was just seventeen and remembers how impressed he had been by an article by Kyffin Williams in *The Studio* and arrived at the School full of Kyffin's words and carrying a palette knife, only to be warned what an evil influence Kyffin Williams. For good measure he was told the palette knife was an abomination.

Crawford ignored the warnings. For Kyffin's 1995 retrospective landscape exhibition he contributed an appreciation of an artist who he confessed had been a great influence, an artist he persuasively compared to Van Gogh:

> There is no doubt that in the post-was period Kyffin Williams is the highest regarded and most successful living Welsh artist in Wales, in terms of both recognition and sales. That is by the public, not the at establishment.
>
> Kyffin played a role both in London and Wales as a traditionalist who put representation before abstraction, certainly emotion and passion before intellect, and the public before the critic. In effect he championed the Expressionist and Romanic over the Conceptualist, but his main concern was not so much against Modern Art as a plea to maintain the value of tradition.
>
> Many feel that Kyffin's depiction of the landscape of Wales embodies the spirit of the place more than any other contemporary artist. If John Piper 'invented' the Welsh chapel, Kyffin invented the farmhouse and the drystone wall. Kyffin's landscape is as sparse as a memory from childhood, ran and re-run in the mind as if it was continually trying to find the answer to a riddle. His landscapes become a metaphor for the Welsh land just as his portraits are a metaphor for the Welsh people.
>
> The artist that Kyffin is clearly closest to, and can most be identified with is Van Gogh, who is probably his real mentor. Stylistically this can best be seen in the similarity of his drawing, which is often conducted in a similar manner to Van Gogh .... comparison is really to be found in the similarity of the psycho-

logical state. Both work with a similar intensity and pace. Both were epileptic... there are great similarities not least in their sensual delight in impasto where pain itself becomes the object of desire. Both artists suffer from the knowledge that intense emotion brings in its wake despair. The despair of failure as an artist. Both take on the landscape and wrestle with it as if one were an angel and the other a devil. Both know that in the relation and reaction to landscape lies their own personality.

His godson Nicholas, whose mother is Kyffin's old love Rosalie Sinclair, is a photographer and not surprisingly an aficionado:

He was the first artist I photographed for a book I plan on British artists. He was incredibly supportive. I feel he is a very contemporary painter although his work fits in with a long British landscape tradition. His work fits into a tradition but he is modern. The use of the palette knife makes his work uniquely identifiable. Imitators never quite pull it off.

His work has grown steadily. Very often an artist peaks and slowly decline as they get older. I think he is producing his best work in the last ten years, the strongest work he has done and particularly the seascapes. The late seascapes are like large abstracts.

The portrait book was my idea. I came up on the last day of the exhibition and said this ought to have been a book, it is madness to have assembled this collection of portraits and not to turn it into a book. He said nothing but when I got home there was a message on my answer phone which said turn right round and come back because you have to photograph the portraits. The Welsh Arts Council were coming up to collect the paintings in three days so we had three very hectic days photographing pictures.

I felt there should be a landscape book which should have come out twenty five years ago. I wrote the introduction, helped in the selection and did all the photographs. They were a fragment of his output. There is enough for four more books.

My mother bought the first picture he sold. It was a small landscape, and now her house is full of them. My christening present was a painting of a nun. So I have had them round me literally since my birth.

He under rates his drawings partly because they come so easily. He is a wonderful cartoonist. He is a wonderful unconventional draughtsman because he is so spontaneous. I think it is important they are more widely recognised. His path through life has been exceptional. Knowing right from the word go that the Welsh landscape was his subject, and he is committed to it. He is the only Welsh artist of the twentieth century of whom this can be said. I went to his studio in London but he must have been a fish out of water. Living in rented rooms must have been hell for him. The move back to Anglesey was very important.

He has an exceptional knowledge of arts history and the contemporary scene. It's tempting to think of him as tucked away in Anglesey. He knows exactly what is going on in the art world and in London. You can ask him about any artist, period or contemporary, and he will know exactly what they are doing. He may not like it but he knows about contemporary art and always argues from the stand point of knowledge.

What happens with the Welsh art establishment is that they have to have a parental role. To take up new young artists and guide them and support them. Kyffin didn't need that. He has always sold. He had an incredibly loyal group. So in a way the Arts Council didn't matter to his career and I think they might have found that difficult to handle.

TEN

In the final decades of his life Kyffin threw himself into the cultural cauldron that is the arts in Wales. Never with more enthusiasm than in the bizarre affair of the Tunnicliffe Bequest with Anglesey Borough Council as an unlikely Medici.

Charles Tunnicliffe was born in 1901, a Cheshire farmer's son who studied etching, engraving and fine art at the Royal College of Art. In the Twenties, he illustrated with incomparable wood engravings, Henry Williamson's classic books *Tarka the Otter* and *Salar the Salmon*. By the 1930s he became an ardent bird watcher. He moved to Anglesey in 1947 and made his home at Malltraeth on the estuary of the Cefni which teems with bird life. Kyffin was a frequent visitor to 'Shorelands', Tunnicliffe's bungalow on the beach and the two became friends. Both men were RAs but their rivalry if it existed at all was never obvious. They were lavish in their praise of each others work.

Tunnicliffe was the more famous of the two outside Wales and in the mid-70's David Robinson, the editorial director of the publishers Gollancz, came up from London to discuss a biography. In Tunnicliffe's studio he spotted a dusty album. Looking idly through it Robinson saw it was a collection of meticulously drawn birds. Tunnicliffe told him it was a collection of measured drawings he had done of dead birds which he had started when his wife brought home a wild duck for supper. "I measured things like wing span and made plumage sketches, studies of bone structure and so on. They are not meant for exhibition. I use them to help me get the birds in my paintings right."

Very much against his will, Tunnicliffe agreed to let Gollancz publish them as a taster to the biography which country author Ian Niall was writing. The biography sold well enough but 90,000 copies of the *Sketchbook of Birds* were sold pre-publication. Although in Bangor, if proof were needed about prophets in their own country it was remaindered. Tunnicliffe died in 1979, before the book came out. Among his papers his executors found two other books, his *Shorelands Winter Diary* and *Shorelands Summer Diary*, both of which were published to a rapturous reception. His works and his royalties went to his sister Dolly, who divided them amongst his eleven nephews and nieces. Somewhere along the way his dying wish that his collection should be kept together at the Royal Academy was lost.

In May 1981 John Smith, an Anglesey fitter with an interest in art, saw that Tunnicliffe's paintings, including the measured drawings which he never wished to be on public show were being auctioned at Christie's. John, who had been a friend of Tunnicliffe's, contacted the leader of Anglesey Council, Elwyn Schofield as a matter of urgency. Smith recalls: "Councils are criticised for being slow to move, but Anglesey Council moved quickly on this one and I will always be grateful to the local authority. I did it through my local councillors and it was delight to see the democratic process working for good."

The council's Chief Executive worked overtime to clinch a deal with the family in the week before the auction. His efforts were successful. For £400,000 the Council became owners of the Tunnicliffe collection. There was a snag. The purchase price did not include the copyright, which might have been expected to have been part of the deal. It was kept by the family which meant that only they have the right to reproduce or franchise the paintings. Thus a very lucrative market which might have recovered the purchase price was lost to Anglesey.

It might have seemed less important to the councillors at the time than keeping the paintings in their home. Unlike most other rural councils Anglesey's coffers were brimming over. The closure of the Suez Canal in 1956 meant that in common with other oil companies, Shell's oil tankers had to make a costly and time consuming voyage round the Horn to their refineries. The answer was to build giant tankers but they brought their own problems. Shell's tankers were consequently too big to sail up to its oil refinery at Ellesmere Port.

Merseyside councils refused the company's offer to build an offshore terminal so Shell turned to Anglesey. At a series of lunches and presentations it offered handsome royalties if the island council would let them build an off shore terminal and also pumping station on the island at Rhosgoch. This the company proposed to transport to Ellesmere Port via twenty-six miles of underground pipes. It would convey a 25 million gallon load through a dazzling piece of engineering, which would bring Anglesey £6,500,000 every eleven years.

Anglesey gratefully accepted, amongst a storm of protest from conservationists. In the event, the Suez Canal re-opened. only limited use was made of the facility and its load never exceeded 10 million gallons. But there was not a single oil spillage and Anglesey was rich, though perhaps not beyond the dreams of avarice. For there was a hidden agenda when the council decided to buy the Tunnicliffe collection. The council was housed in a ramshackle series of huts and prefabricated buildings which surrounded the main headquarters. An inner cabinet met and decided to include the gallery which would house the collection in a larger scheme which would include council offices, courts and county council buildings. The gallery would cost £300,000 a year to run and need a staff of seven.

The present writer heard of the scheme and wrote a story which appeared in the *Sunday Mirror* which included criticisms from other councillors. When the plan of the inner cabinet for a three phase building programme at a total cost of £8 million was presented to the council it was thrown out.

Kyffin had been delighted when the council bought the Tunnicliffe suggestion but dismayed when he read of the it's plan. He hurried to offer an alternative suggestion. 'Shorelands' had been bought by a couple who found it inconvenient. They were ready to sell for £90,000. Part of it could be used to house the collection with another part adapted as a flat for a 'Resident bird artist' to look after it. In the event, his was one of twenty-five inexpensive alternatives ranging from Llanfairpwll station to Presaddfed, a mansion at Bodedern. None was accepted.

At about this time the council was visited by Jaap Klootwijk, Shell UK's managing director, to tell them the agreement would only last until 1988 and the company could not go on making annual payments of £600,000. Yet the council was undeterred. It was suggested that if there was not enough oil revenue to maintain the gallery, a merchant bank could be approached for a loan.

Kyffin led a protest movement which included twenty-five local and cash starved Anglesey community councils. For eight years the arguments went on and for several of those years the Tunnicliffe collection was stored in a cellar at the National Gallery in Cardiff. It seemed as though there would never be a place to house it, although curiously a director was appointed for the gallery which did not exist. Four years after the paintings were purchased, and another four years before a much less ambitious gallery was opened at Llangefni, Denise (Black) Morris, an award winning curator, was head hunted from Scunthorpe. It proved a brilliant choice. From the moment it opened in 1998 Oriel Ynys Mon was an outstanding success under her inspired leadership.

She and Kyffin quickly became allies. He worked tirelessly for the gallery. In 1990 he donated the gallery 293 drawings – and the copyright — to the gallery. Even then they were estimated to be worth well over £10,000 and their value has increased handsomely since. Under Mrs Morris's guidance the gallery won a clutch of awards and put on exhibitions by local artists which gave the gallery the best attendance in North Wales, and it has become among the best galleries in the whole of the Principality.

Alas, Denise Morris got little support for the council and when under local government reorganisation in Anglesey became a county authority her application for the post of Director of Leisure was turned down and went instead to Elspeth Mitcheson, the former Director of Leisure for Gwynedd. In 1998 relations between the two women had become so bad that Denise Morris felt that she could not work there any longer. The council accepted her resignation with no show of regret.

Kyffin was incensed. From that day onwards he refused to visit the gallery and cancelled plans to have his eightieth birthday retrospective exhibition there. When at the end of the year Mrs Morris took Anglesey Council to an industrial tribunal with an unsuccessful claim for wrongful constructive dismissal Kyffin paid her considerable legal fees with a collection of judicial caricatures he had drawn. Such quiet acts of kindness were typical of him.

It was in 1998, too, that a Kyffin painting appeared on the *Antiques Roadshow* which was valued by the expert Rupert Maas at £14,000. Mr Mars said, "The market must in years to come recognise Kyffin Williams as an important artist. There is something about him that captures exactly the colours and tones of his country. This painting contains many different shades of the same colour. It ranges from khaki through slate grey to brilliant green. I like particularly the slabby painting technique and the greys of the slate slabs. It is all caught marvellously. He shares with Constable the ability to catch a landscape."

In the same year a painting of a Welsh Black bull, owned by O.G. Thomas, he President of the Royal Welsh Show was auctioned at the show for £7,000. A set of 150 signed prints of an Anglesey cottage which he donated to the National Eisteddfod to commemorate its visit to Anglesey in 1999 raised £12,000 for Eisteddfod funds.

What pleased him most, though was the support he got from a powerful figure in the British establishment, the Liberal Democrat peer Lord Hooson QC. At the launch of the £40 a copy *Land and Sea* book, a collection of Kyffin's land and seascapes, at the National Library of Wales, Lord Hooson stated that Kyffin was one of the outstanding artist to emerge in Wales over the last half century. He went on:

> He is an uncompromising man, finds little to his taste in the dictates of either mediocrity or the establishment and he has made it his business to improve the institutional situation in terms of professionalism and the status of Welsh work in Wales. His complete independence, both in his painting and his various battles with institutions, has led to a different view of art being taken and has contributed greatly to the more favourable environment in which gradually younger artists are able to work in Wales
>
> No man was ever truer to himself than Kyffin. It is this engaging individualism that so endears him to the people of Wales and enables him to relate to them and they to him in a way few poets, or musicians even, have been able to achieve.
>
> Every now and then Wales throws up somebody who in his or

her way and in a particular art form communicates with the nation. William Williams Pantycelyn was one. Dafydd ap Gwilym was another. Ann Griffiths another. It would not surprise me that in the future, as for so many of us now, Kyffin is able, like them, to communicate with the inner soul of Wales.

Let me conclude by saying the launch of this book enables us to acknowledge our great appreciation first of all of Kyffin the man – his indomitable spirit, his enhancement of our appreciation of our country, of our people and of our idiosyncrasies. We also salute him as a truly Welsh artist with an international appeal and possibly, by establishments, more appreciated outside Wales than in. But an artist to whom the people of Wales relate.

No man, surely, had a better epitaph.

EPILOGUE

Kyffin was the oddest invalid I have ever met. Though genuinely suffering from a multiplicity of ailments, he nonetheless managed to hunt with the Snowdon pack, drive endless distances without any evidence of tiredness, walk miles and climb mountains I could only watch through half-closed fingers. He was impervious to cold. Indeed, when he was painting, he was impervious to anything.

Inevitably the years took their toll and by his eighties he was beginning to flag. I moved from Wales, so for two years I did not see him. I loved Anglesey so much and missed it so badly I could not bear to go back, though we kept in touch by phone and letter. When eventually I did steel myself and returned to Llanfairpwll to stay with his neighbours and friends, the Reverend Peter Gledhill and his wife Bridget, Kyffin came to dinner clutching a lovingly inscribed book of his portraits.

I was shocked when I saw him. For the first time he looked old and unwell. His spirit, though, was unaffected. That evening he sparkled with outrageous anecdotes and hurled verbal thunderbolts at Britart, art schools and painters who could not draw. Peter was a scholarly man, whom we both loved dearly, and Kyffin and I had a private game to see who could be the first with an outrageous remark to make him rub his head and say, with great gravity, "I am afraid I cannot quite agree with that."

Kyffin was the ideal dinner guest. He could even make R.S. Thomas laugh. We had another private joke. I told him he was kept alive by the chicken casserole which coursed through his veins, the product of a convoy of concerned women who brought delicious dishes down the pitted lane to his house by the sea, concerned he wasn't getting enough to eat. Enough? He dined out

most nights, once a week with us before we moved away, once
with the Marquess and Marchioness of Anglesey; weekends
would find him being pampered to death by Annwen and Bengy
Carey-Evans at their home in Criccieth. He may have been
Wales's greatest painter – I am biased and, anyway, not competent
to judge – but he was certainly Wales's most loved man.

When I returned to the scenery-free Fens, the letters and the
phone calls continued but they were not as frequent. When his
Kyffin in Venice book was published, my wife Celia bought it for
my birthday in May. Kyffin and I were both born on Ascension
Day. Kyffin insisted this entitled us to two birthdays. She wrote to
Kyffin to ask for a letter to paste in the front. When the reply
came, it was written by Denise Morris, the first director at Oriel
Ynys Mon, a constant friend and carer to Kyffin whom she
revered. The letter read:

> Dear Celia
> I am fully conscious of the proximity of the birthday of Ian and
> myself but I am afraid I am unable to mark the auspicious date
> by writing a suitable inscription. The reason for this is that I can
> no longer write, even though I am able to draw a bit somehow.
> Strange but there we are.
> Denise is writing this for me, as she does for all those who get
> in touch with me. I am very lucky.
> Do let me know if you are coming down here again. I always
> enjoy seeing you.
> Love,
> Kyffin
> (dictated to Denise)

Denise had added a note: "Kyffin is very weak and tires
quickly. He could hardly raise the breath to dictate this letter, but
I am hoping he will be stronger soon."

Alarmed, I wrote at once and this reply came:

> Dear Ian
> I was very touched to get your letter. My battle with bogey goes
> on. The medical people are very kind and they are pulling out all
> the stops. I am also grateful to all my friends round here who
> cannot seem to do enough for me.
> I am so glad you are settling down in March. It must have
> been difficult for you – just as I couldn't leave here.

As for the Buddhism, I am delighted to think it is helping you. It has always been very attractive to Welsh people and there have been a lot of well known Buddhists. I could have been a Buddhist, I think, as I could well have been a vegetarian.

It was good to hear from you and Celia. We must keep in touch.

Love,
Kyffin"

Again Denise had added a note: "Kyffin is getting very weak but is in good enough spirits as you can see by his letter. His oncologist has put in for a new drug for him so we are all trying for optimism."

Soon after came the phone call we had dreaded. It was from another friend Father Brian Jones, who, with Dr Margaret Wood, had frequently entertained Kyffin to some of Margaret's epicurean meals at their cottage in Llansadwrn, a cottage which Kyffin had painted a picture of it in his youth. It now hangs on their wall.

Kyffin once described himself as "an obsessive, depressive, diabetic epileptic". Some years ago, prostate cancer (and later lung cancer) joined the enemy fighting for his body. Kyffin reacted with wry humour. He was treated by the legendary consultant Miss Evans at Bodelwyddan Hospital, a lady, he told me, who had seen every notable backside (and private parts) in Wales. She was the recipient of some of his finest cartoons and poems.

In August 2006, the cancer had him on the ropes. He was taken to Ysbyty Gwynedd and two weeks later transferred to St Tysilio Nursing Home, less than a mile from his home on the Straits, where on Friday, September 1, he died. The Marquess of Anglesey told me that the day he died, Kyffin, to everyone's surprise, ate a hearty breakfast of bacon and eggs.

On Monday, September 11, the man who once expected a quiet funeral in a country church had what amounted in Wales to a State Funeral, conducted by another friend, the Archbishop of Wales, Dr Barry Morgan. The Prince of Wales, who had invited Kyffin to Highgrove to show him his paintings, was represented by the Lord Lieutenant of Gwynedd, Huw Daniel.

The coffin was draped with white roses and dark red carnations, and 600 people, most of whom knew and loved him, packed Bangor Cathedral for the hour-long service of thanksgiving for his life and work. His godson Nicholas Sinclair paid a tribute to the man who thought of him as the son he never had; a second tribute came from Professor Derec Llwyd Morgan, the former Principal of Aberystwyth University. The Lesson was read by the Marquess of Anglesey and a favourite psalm by Father Brian Jones.

It came as no surprise that Kyffin had planned his own service to the last ecumenical detail. It was his final work of art. Bryn Terfel sang one of Kyffin's favourite songs 'My Little Welsh Home', accompanied by harpist Elinor Bennett. The Ynys Mon AM Ieuan Wyn Jones commented: "It was absolutely amazing, absolutely wonderful. We had one great artist singing to another."

Professor Morgan, who comes from Anglesey, is chairman of the Kyffin Williams Trust that has been established to plan the gallery within a gallery at Oriel Ynys Mon, dedicated to Kyffin's work. In his tribute he explained the one luxury that Kyffin permitted himself, a Volvo motor car. Kyffin had called in at his local Volvo dealers to pick up his morning newspaper. A girl in the salesroom told him she had just the car for him, with a YSK registration. She said it stood for 'Young Sir Kyffin'. He bought it on the spot.

The Archbishop of Wales, a former bishop of Bangor, said that the fact the cathedral was full of people from all walks of society was testimony to the esteem in which Kyffin was held – not just as an artist, but as a man. "We have come out of respect and to give thanks for him. But we are only able to do so because he, in the end, consented to have a service such as this. His preferred option was a quiet burial at Llanfairynghornwy. A quiet burial because he himself was self deprecating about his work. 'Not much talent really,' he once said."

In the end, as he always did, Kyffin got his way. He was buried in the tiny churchyard at Llanfairynghornwy. He would have been amazed: outwardly horrified, but secretly pleased, by the explosion of tributes which followed his death.

The *Daily Telegraph* obituarist drew attention to his life in London:

For the next thirty years (1944-73) the post at Highgate provided Williams with the perfect base to develop his highly characteristic work, "free from the pressures of fashion and the contagious influences of art schools".

The school, it has to be said, was extraordinarily tolerant. Williams's increasingly frequent truancies on nearby Hampstead Heath generated only gentle rebukes from the headmaster ("By the way, you didn't turn up for a lesson. You know, it is awfully difficult if you don't"), and he was actually appointed senior art master; over the years he was much loved by his pupils, and he produced some outstanding students.

Williams was fortunate in that, despite his medical problems, he had extraordinary physical energy. He could fulfil his teaching duties while producing something like 100 paintings a year.

The evolution of his characteristic style is something of a paradox. By temperament very much a conservative, Williams was always in a state of war with the authorities, promoting contemporary art in Wales – he wanted to found a gallery for the history of Welsh art, but wanted it to stop at 1950 when, in his view, all the problems of modern art began.

But the manner in which he began to paint owed a great deal to just those aspects of modern art with which he professed to be so uncomfortable.

With his bold palette-knife application of paint, sombre tonality and considerable degree of abstraction, Williams pursued an artistic path far removed from the kind of well-mannered, painterly sub-Impressionism in which such attitudes usually resulted; it was a path closer, in fact, to the dark-hued Expressionism of the early twentieth century paintings of peasant life by the Belgian artist Constant Permeke.

Williams's choice of direction was not, perhaps, so mysterious. His brief employment as a land agent before the war had made him very familiar with the landscape of Snowdonia and, more specifically, with the hill-farmers who lived and worked there and had helped shape its present-day appearance.

Nothing better captures Williams the man than his friendship with the great natural history artist Charles Tunnicliffe. A near-neighbour of Tunnicliffe on Anglesey for many years, Williams persuaded the Royal Academy to put on an exhibition of Tunnicliffe's unique collection of measured drawings and sketchbooks of birds in 1974.

He once described himself as "an obsessive, depressive, diabetic epileptic, who's apprehensive, selfish, intolerant and ruthless". It is a harsh self-assessment from a man who was not only warm and funny but also extremely generous of his time

and energy on behalf of other artists.
Kyffin Williams never married.

Betsan Powys, then BBC Wales arts and media correspondent, recalled that Kyffin said he spent a lifetime responding to the landscape and the people of the area in which he grew up. She told listeners:

> His subject matter never strayed far from the landscape where his family had been for generations.
> "I never had to think what shall I paint," he once said. "I don't think how I should paint it. The whole thing to me somehow is far too natural a thing. It is there and I am the vehicle for expressing it."
> Sir Kyffin was, by his own admission, an obsessive and a pessimist whose turbulent inner life was reflected in the heavy oils he applied with a palette knife and in the sombre mountains that he painted.
> Some criticised him for using too much black in his work.
> But that, he said, was how he saw things.
> "I paint for kicks rather like Van Gogh painted for kicks – excitement. Maybe if you're an epileptic you crave excitement.
> "And I wanted the excitement of a strong dark against the bright light. It does something for me like other people take alcohol".
> He claimed to have no idea why people were prepared to pay tens of thousands of pounds for his work. One oil painting – 'A Hill Farmer and his Dog' – was sold for £48,000 at an auction in May this year (2006).
> Kyffin Williams said he always had a horror of having to stop painting his 'cynefin' – his own patch of North Wales. "I sometimes feel the last canvas I have covered is the last canvas I will ever cover," he told the BBC in 1999, "but then I go and paint another one and so it goes on".

The *Times* obituary was equally warm and generous:

> Sir Kyffin Williams was a portraitist, a painter of North Welsh landscapes and seascapes, and an amused chronicler of his own and other people's foibles.
> Rain-lashed, green-grey landscapes, stormy, slate-grey seascapes and weather-beaten, pink-grey farmers are the recurring themes of Williams's art, sketched and, in many cases, painted outdoors in his beloved North Wales.
> There was never anything precious about Williams's attitude

to his art. One of his trademarks was that he would knead and model his oil paints with a palette knife, regardless of whether or not this was fashionable with the art establishment (and it was not). "You can use a pair of nail scissors or hose pipes. But a palette knife? No. It's incredible the rules they have," he told *Artists & Illustrators* magazine this year.

He was an unassuming man, only too happy for an oil he was painting to be inadvertently improved by its toppling, face down, on to his new tweed hat, or for the texture of a watercolour, being tackled al fresco on the windy shore of Llanddwyn, to be helped along by the addition of wind-blown sand.

Williams had a way with words as well. His autobiography, *Across the Straits* (1973), immortalises in print his skills as a raconteur as he decries his own tennis ability (his forehand drive "was practically unreturnable and certainly if it was returned I was so surprised that I lost the point") or is astonished by the high-handedness of a certain Lord Davies, who decided when everyone in Llandinam should be in bed by turning the master switch that plunged the village into darkness "at an annoyingly early hour."

Crucially, the teaching of drawing was one of the Slade's great strengths, and as Williams wrote in his 2001 book, *Drawings*: "Paintings are often laboured things, and when worked upon over a period of time they tend to lose the initial excitement of conception. Drawings are usually fresh; they tell us much about the artist who created them."

A generous supporter of his local community, he gave drawing lessons in Gwynedd primary schools; judged, and donated the main prize for a Welsh national drawing competition; and served as patron of the Bardsey Island Trust, whose protection of that island's wildlife and ecosystem was a cause close to his heart. And he regularly donated drawings and prints to be auctioned for local causes...

Having selected art for the National Eisteddfod of Wales several times between 1955 and 1989, in later years Williams became exasperated with some of the works receiving awards there (as indeed he did with winners of the Turner Prize). In 2005, when the Eisteddfod's fine-art medal was won by a video installation showing people in combat fatigues burning a garden shed, he was not alone in thinking it was "like awarding the championship in the Welsh Black cattle class to a sheep".

If anything, his new "grumpy old man" image boosted his popularity beyond his already very wide circle of friends. He had been knighted in 2000, but in 2006 there was a tribute of another kind from James Dean Bradfield, frontman of the Welsh rock band, the Manic Street Preachers. A track called 'Which Way To Kyffin?' featured on Bradfield's debut album as a solo artist, and was explained thus by the rock star, fifty years Williams's junior: "I was in West Wales last year and I had this feeling where I didn't want to go back to London and was really fighting not to go back. I just felt like driving up to Anglesey to find Kyffin Williams."

More locally, in the *Daily Post*, David Greenwood focussed on Kyffin's relationship with Anglesey:

> Sir Kyffin's death comes as major efforts were being stepped up to build a "gallery within a gallery" at Oriel Ynys Mon to house his works. Sir Kyffin, who lived and had his studio at Llanfairpwll overlooking the Menai Strait, had even backed a major fund-raising by promoting the sale of signed prints of his work.
>
> But last night Anglesey's museums and culture officer Alun Gruffydd said efforts to build the gallery would continue. He said: "Naturally, everyone associated with Oriel Ynys Mon has been saddened by the news of Sir Kyffin's death.
>
> "He was the most renowned artist of his generation and became a leading figure in the campaign for the development and the establishment of Oriel Ynys Mon. He generously donated over 400 original works of art to the gallery and we will continue our quest to build a fitting gallery extension in his name to display this collection of work. Such a gallery extension would be an appropriate celebration of his immense contribution to the arts here in Anglesey and nationally."

There were personal tributes, too. Edward Pari-Jones, who runs Oriel Gwyngyll, a fine arts gallery in Llanfairpwll, had known Sir Kyffin for thirty years. He said: "He was almost Edwardian in character, always encouraging young artists. He was a very giving person. He was an icon of sorts. People loved his work and there were some detractors as well. I last saw him a few weeks ago when I called at his home. He wasn't very well."

Vicky MacDonald, former curator of the Royal Cambrian Academy who worked with Sir Kyffin when he was president for twelve years, described him as charismatic: "What can you say about one of Wales' greatest ever artists. A private view would light up when he walked in. People would be enthralled just talking and listening to him. As a person he was a delight, so kind and gentle but not afraid to speak his mind."

And author and broadcaster David Meredith wrote in the *Daily Post*:

> Kyffin Williams, Sir Kyffin or, as he preferred, just Kyffin, was without question for me Wales' greatest artist, an artistic giant undertaking his chosen profession of "making a living by painting" with determination, perseverance and discipline.
>
> He also believed in the old adage "keep your friendships in repair." How privileged I was to be able to regard him as a friend – and he had a great many.
>
> Kyffin believed in passion, love and obsession as being vital to good art and that obsession – "something deep down" – was more important than talent even. He certainly imbued all his painting with love, his love of the mountains of Gwynedd, and the sea as it crashed on the shores of his native Anglesey. And he was certainly obsessed with portraying the farmers of Wales, his fellow countrymen, who cared for the land and their stock with equal care and attention.
>
> Kyffin was a multi-talented artist, a painter in oil and watercolour, ink wash and pencil, a brilliant book illustrator as we saw in his Gregynog publications; his Crawshay Bailey cartoons abound with humour.

In the *Western Mail*, Tryst Williams drew attention to Kyffin's relationships with other artists:

> Former Young Artist of the Year Dan Llywelyn Hall was one of many artists to pay generous tribute to the Anglesey-born painter who died on Friday, aged 88. He said, "No single artist has touched on the Welsh psyche as profoundly as Kyffin Williams. His art has helped to shape and define the nation's visual identity. He touched on the melancholy of the landscape and the contradiction of the exhilaration and isolation that we can sometimes experience.
>
> "As an artist, I admired his dedication to his subject matter and his tireless efforts to promote Welsh art to an international audience – like few have before him. His palette of colour was distinctly Welsh and he somehow managed to describe the landscape in the most succinct and economical of ways.
>
> "For me his portraits probed even deeper exposing human struggle and a certain grit to his subjects. I wrote to Kyffin on many occasions sending samples of recent work including a

portrait I'd not long ago completed of Cliff Morgan. He always responded with insightful comments and suggestions of how to progress.

He often helped to describe the difficulties faced whilst living as an artist and how he'd overcome them in his lifetime. It was encouraging to hear how a healthy obsession in your art can outlive most worldly problems. I'm sure he was a mentor to many artists alike, almost a father figure of the passing generation of Welsh artists. I'm sure his work will live on to tell the tale."

Works by Sir Kyffin which had already been offered for sale on internet auction site eBay received a flurry of bids in the wake of his death. One vendor was even offering a copy of Saturday's *Western Mail*, featuring news of Sir Kyffin's death, for sale at £8.99.

Meanwhile Wales' richest artist called on the Assembly to help save Sir Kyffin's work for the nation. Andrew Vicari, who was official painter for the Saudi Arabian Government, said a permanent exhibition of his art should be put on display immediately. The pair were long-time friends and were due to paint each others' portraits next year.

Vicari said, "Kyffin was one of nature's greatest gentlemen – a great artist and a great friend. "I hope that Wales, for once, tries to do something marvellous to commemorate the superb work of one of its most famous, and favourite, sons. There are statues to great sportsmen, museums dedicated to ancient artefacts, but the majority of the nation's art treasures are stored away where nobody can see them. I would urge the Assembly to find some way to purchase for the nation as many of Kyffin's treasures as possible."

Ironically, during his lifetime, Sir Kyffin had himself campaigned tirelessly for a Welsh National Art Gallery to be set up.

★ ★ ★

Typically, Kyffin's will was thoughtful and generous in its bequests. He left £500,000 to charities and other deserving bodies. In addition, the National Library of Wales was given his art collection, which ran to approximately 250 oils on canvas, 600 watercolours and drawings, diaries, photographs and slides, original manuscripts of books by Kyffin and several sketchbooks. Among them is a painting of St Jerome by the Italian artist Domenichino which is currently being valued and could be worth around £1 million. Further paintings were bequeathed to the

University of Wales at Bangor and to the National Museum of Wales.

Among the beneficiaries of his estate (valued at more than £6 million) are the bodies with which he was closely associated like the Royal Cambrian Academy of Art in Conwy, and the fine book press Gwasg Gregynog, each of which receive £100,000. The Council for the Protection of Rural Wales – the subject of Kyffin's art – the Tabernacl Arts Centre in Machynlleth, the Ucheldre Arts Centre in Holyhead, on Anglesey, and the Artists' Benevolent Fund (which supports the widows of artists) also received substantial bequests.

Index

---

to *The Astonishing Infantry* 118;
Mabinogion 118; *Patagonia Revisited*
118; *Two Old Men* 118; *Welsh
Anthology* 118
and brother 34-6, 87, 92
cartoons 98, 121, 128, 138, 144
childhood 10-42
christened John 7
education 38-42, 88
family tree 7, 8, 9, 26-38, 108-9
generosity 50-3, 113-4, 133, 145-6
and Gwynedd mountains 8, 10, 11,
98, 110, 141
and the Home Guard 54, 61, 64-5, 68
receives honours 7, 107, 118, 119
love of hunting and shooting 8, 10-15,
25, 55, 63, 89-90
illnesses: epilepsy 8, 9, 49-53, 56, 59,
62, 91, 121, 127-8; others 8, 49, 52,
136-8
lives on Anglesey 107-35
relationship with mother 11
visits Patagonia 100, 101-6, 119
portrait painting 23, 67, 98, 99, 111-3,
134
and Royal Academy 7, 88, 91, 100,
107, 118, 122
attends Slade School of Art 57-60, 61-
2, 63-8, 82, 123
and teaching 7, 68-75, 91, 140
and Welsh art 90-1, 94-7, 114, 115,
144, 145
Welshness 7, 53, 97-8, 129, 135
and women 54, 56, 60-3, 78-80, 91-2,
116-7, 136

Williams, Louisa 41
Williams Llion 94-6, 97-8
Williams, Mary 'Mamie' (*aunt*) 31, 39
Williams, Maggie 113
Williams, Nanny 36
Williams, Owen, 26
Williams, Owen (grandson of Thomas)
28
Williams, Owen (*grandfather*) 29
Williams, Prys 21

Williams, Richard (*brother*) 8, 9, 13,
24-5, 33-6, 39, 49, 50, 66, 87, 92
Williams, Richard 22
Williams, Rosalie 60-1, 80, 84, 128
Williams, Thomas (son of Owen) 27-8
Williams, Tom (*great uncle*) 30-1
Williams, Tryst 144
Williams, Wendy Wynn 22
Williams, William 'Pantycelyn' 135
Williams Wynn family 22
Williams Bank 22
Williams-Bulkeley, Sir Richard 38
Williams-Ellis, Clough 15, 20
Williamson, Henry: *Salar the Salmon*
130; *Tarka the Otter* 130
Windermere Foot Harriers 21
Windmill Theatre 75
Wmffre ap William John ap Rhys 26
Wolverhampton University 122
Wood., Dr Margaret 138
Wrexham 47-8
Wynn, Denise 46
Wynn, Fred 45-6
Wynn, Ruby 45
Wynn, Thomas John (fifth Baron
Newborough) 45-6
Wynn, Vaughan 45-6
Wynne- Williams, Michael 78, 79
Wynne-Williams, Valerie (née Price)
78-80

Yale & Hardcastle 43-4
Yale, George Frederick Cunngham 44
Yapp, Mary 8,
Afon Ynysfor 16
Ynyfor (house) 24
Ynysfor Hunt 11, 12-5, 16, 18-9, 20,
21, 22-3, 25
Ynys Mawr 11
Ysbyty Gwynedd 114, 138
Ysbyty Gwynedd Epilespy Group 51-2

THE AUTHOR

Ian Skidmore is the author of thirty books: histories, biographies, fiction and comedy, yet left school aged 12. He first visited Gwynedd two years prior to that, on holiday, and returned to live within sight of it on Anglesey for many years. A former *Daily Mirror* journalist, and a columnist elsewhere, he later became a broadcaster for Radio Wales and other stations, with a weekly audience of 26 million worldwide. He was awarded a Golden Microphone for Services to Broadcasting and the accolade "One of that rare breed of radio men to have that old BBC asset, real charm on air" from Peter Florence, Director of the Hay Festival. A neighbour and friend of Kyffin Williams on Anglesey, he lives now in East Anglia.